DANGER
C A L L I N G

DANGER
CALLING

TRUE ADVENTURES OF RISK AND FAITH

YOUTH EDITION

PEB JACKSON
JAMES LUND

Revell

a division of Baker Publishing Group
Grand Rapids, Michigan

Published by Revell
a division of Baker Publishing Group
P.O. Box 6287, Grand Rapids, MI 49516-6287
www.revellbooks.com

Printed in the United States of America

Library of Congress Cataloging-in-Publication Data
Jackson, Peb.
    Danger calling : true adventures of risk and faith / Peb Jackson, James Lund.
— Youth ed.
        p.   cm.
    Includes bibliographical references.
    ISBN 978-0-8007-3405-3 (pbk.)
        1. Christian youth—Religious life. 2. Risk taking (Psychology)—Religious aspects—Christianity. 3. Adventure and adventurers. I. Lund, James L. II. Title.
    BV4531.3.J34 2010
    248.4—dc22   2010013622

Published in association with William K. Jensen Literary Agency, 119 Bampton Court, Eugene, Oregon 97404.

10 11 12 13 14 15 16   7 6 5 4 3 2 1

To my longtime friend Tim Hansel and the gang at Summit Expedition, who fired me up in countless ways, especially in reference to mountains and great effort.

Peb

To my children, Erik, Sonja, and Peter—may you follow the Lord's calling wherever it leads.

Jim

Contents

Part Four: Leadership

Acknowledgments

Most of my pursuits of adventure and opportunities in the wild were inspired by friends and by books. I vividly recall leafing through a coffee table book, *The Earth and Great Weather*. I found a picture of a canyon with steep walls above the Arctic Circle that mesmerized me—a dramatic vista indeed. I said, "I am going there someday." Ten years later, I was tromping through that exact canyon in the Brooks Range in Alaska. All of my expectations were exceeded. That scenario has been repeated many times over the past decades and I am sure will be duplicated in years to come.

A bookmark that my friend Scott McOwen and I had made for Guttenberg's, a bookstore we built, had as its tagline, "A man can't have too many books or too many friends." I have been powerfully motivated, inspired, and blessed by an abundance of both.

I want to acknowledge my partner in this venture, Jim Lund, and the indefatigable nature of this guy's disciplined conscientiousness in his writing. What a gift he has been to me in the re-creation and telling of these marvelous stories. Thank you, Jim.

To my wife, Sharon, who still flinches when I talk about ice climbing or any such pursuits, but at least has not attached a tether to my ankle . . . yet. But in reality she is my consistent, joyful partner, adventuring through this life.

Peb

Some people are called not only to dangerous adventures in life and faith but also to generously share their time, stories, and insights with pesky writers. This book would not have been possible without the help and patience of, among others, Eric Alexander, B. J. Kramps, Leon Lamprecht, Melissa Neugebauer, Todd Pierce, Dick Savidge, Drew Wills, Jeanie Wills, and my partner in publishing, the incomparable Peb Jackson. My deep thanks to each of you.

Thanks also go to our agent, Bill Jensen, the man with a million great ideas; to our editor, Andrea Doering, who patiently steered us home; and to everyone at Baker Publishing Group who played a part in enabling us to present these stories.

To Jon Coulter and the Sisters Young Life study group, thanks for the "test run." To Gil McCormick for your insights and encouragement and to Jodi Carroll for all that you do. I appreciate it.

A special word of gratitude goes to Tom Stoerzbach for invaluable research and writing assistance. Tom, you saved the day.

Last and certainly not least, I thank my family for their encouragement and support: my wife, Angela; my children, Erik, Sonja, and Peter; and my brother, Dave, who also contributed research and writing help. You guys are the best.

Jim

Introduction

This isn't your typical Bible study. We're going to take you on a high-adrenaline ride to places few people dare to go—the thin air at the peak of Mount Everest, the black waters at the bottom of the Atlantic, the steaming jungles of the Philippines, and the frozen floes of the Antarctic. We'll also take you to a few other places just as dangerous and exciting—the depths of your heart, life, and faith.

Danger Calling is a book of true stories. It features people in extreme situations, often brought on by their own extreme choices. Some stories will be familiar. Some have never been told before. All will keep you in suspense, with lives hanging on every decision.

This is also a book of questions. We're going to challenge you to think about your response to each story and what it means to you. You'll find no pat answers. We'll explore four primary themes—courage, sacrifice, perseverance, and leadership—with questions such as these: *Would you give up your life jacket to save another person on a sinking ship? How much are you willing to risk for fame and glory? What is your source of strength in a crisis? Could you lead a friend out of danger after a plane crash in the mountains?*

Especially when you're young, it can be hard to know where you fit in and what you're supposed to do next. Part of our goal is to help you with that—to enable you to discover who you are. But we also want you to find out who you're meant to be. We see this as a matter of faith, and we want you to know where you stand. Through this book, we're asking: *Do you have a relationship with God? Are you a little too comfortable in your faith? Is he calling you to a life of greater risk and deeper meaning?*

We are a couple of guys who are fascinated by the often-hidden benefits of risk and danger and how they connect to faith. Peb is the true adventurer. As a boy, he scaled the ten-story water tower in his hometown of Haviland, Kansas (unroped). He's been testing his limits on mountains, bike trails, rapids, and jungle safaris ever since. Jim is the writer who can't decide which he loves more—a great hike in the wilderness or a great story about one. We had a good time joining forces on our first book of adventure stories, *A Dangerous Faith*. We wanted to go further, to reach into people's hearts and lead them to their calling. Inspired by conversations with our agent, Bill Jensen, we began talking about a new project that would challenge people to think about their lives and faith. We want to invite you into an adventure that's as old as our existence: "Seek me and live" (Amos 5:4). The result is in your hands.

How you approach *Danger Calling* is up to you. The sixteen stories and follow-up questions are designed for talking over with a few friends, but you can certainly tackle them in a larger group, with just one friend, or on your own. The idea is to read one story before you meet with your group and then go through the follow-up material for that story. *Would You? Could You?* features probing questions and relevant Scripture passages. Use it to think about what you want to say to the group. As you go through it, write down other verses to share and discuss. *Reporting In* is your invitation to connect with the Lord through prayer, either as a group or individually. *Hitting the Trail* is a section just for you, an opportunity to write down and apply whatever you're learning.

New Territory lists more questions and books, videos, and other resources to explore when you want to dig deeper.

When you meet with your group, be honest and open about your ideas and doubts. You won't get much out of this book if you say only what others want to hear. Remember to give everyone a chance to share, and encourage each other to tell your own stories of danger and faith. Allow time to thoroughly discuss each question. Feel free to take on more than one story in a session. And once you're done with *Danger Calling*, don't just throw it away. Wait a few months or a year, then go through it again. You may be surprised by how much your life and faith have changed.

You won't always be comfortable with the questions in this book—or your answers. That's okay. You're starting a daring adventure, and risk and adventure are never easy. The Lord designed it that way. He uses our struggles and our proximity to danger to draw us closer to him. We find him on that precarious ridge between the comfortable and the unknown. It's where we need to be. It's the place where we discover that the more we risk and trust God, the closer we move to his heart and the higher calling for which he created us.

Thank you for joining us on this journey. Are you ready? It's time to dive deeper into danger and nearer to the Author of the greatest adventure of all.

PART ONE

COURAGE

1

Fear and Friendship at the Top of the World

> The LORD will watch over your coming and
> going both now and forevermore.
>
> Psalm 121:8

Eric Alexander pauses on a near-vertical slope to kick ice off his crampons and gulp another mouthful of oxygen-depleted air. He's thrilled to be here—twenty-two thousand feet above sea level, ascending the western flank of Lhotse that leads to the peak of Mount Everest. But he's also concerned. The Lhotse face is difficult under any circumstances, but this season, as the ice and snow melt, it's raining down a frightening amount of debris.

And Eric has more than his own neck to worry about. The thirty-two-year-old is part of a team that hopes to guide his friend and fellow climber, Erik Weihenmayer, to Everest's summit. Weihenmayer is attempting to become the first blind person to reach the top of the world.

Eric has led his friend most of the morning. He has a bell attached to his pack so Weihenmayer can follow the sound, and he calls out instructions such as "Deep crevasse here—you gotta jump all the way across" and "Chunky ice here—you need to raise your right leg high." Now, however, he's about two hundred feet above Weihenmayer and his teammates.

Suddenly, something dark, about the size of a softball, hurtles past Eric.

"Rock!" he yells, a warning to those below. To his horror, he sees the missile is headed straight for Weihenmayer.

Even if he could see it coming, Weihenmayer would have no time to dodge. He freezes. The rock slams into the snow at his feet and bounces down the slope.

Whoa, that was close, Eric thinks. *Thank goodness it didn't hit him. Let's move!*

The team has nearly reached camp 3 at 23,500 feet when Eric stops to check his heart rate. After the stress of hauling a big load to camp 2 the day before, it was high all night. Now he finds it's still high: over 180 beats a minute. Reluctantly, Eric decides he's pushed himself too hard; he needs to reduce altitude. After a conversation with Weihenmayer, he turns around and begins retracing his path on the icy Lhotse face back to camp 2. Five minutes later, as he picks his way down an especially steep slope, he's satisfied he's made the hard but right decision.

His thoughts are interrupted by a strange thumping sound from above. He looks up. A boulder the size of a truck tire is hurtling straight at him. It's less than one hundred feet away.

Eric's reaction is instinctive. He tucks his head and makes two quick hops to his left.

Is it enough?

The boulder flies past, missing Eric by inches. If he'd stayed in position, he'd very likely be dead.

Eric draws one long, deep breath. Then he drops to one knee on the slope.

Lord, please keep me safe the rest of the way down.
He continues his descent at a much quicker pace.

The manager of a mountaineering shop in Vail, Colorado, and a devoted climber, Eric met Weihenmayer through his roommate in late 1997 and found they had similar interests in climbing. Soon they were joining forces on increasingly difficult ice climbs in Colorado. Weihenmayer's lack of vision barely slowed him down. Eric realized it was more inconvenience than obstacle.

On another climb with Weihenmayer, one question changed Eric's future. "I've got this idea to climb Everest," Weihenmayer said. "I'm putting some friends together, and I think you'd be a good addition to the team. What do you think?"

For Eric, it was the opportunity to achieve a lifelong dream, one he never expected to fulfill. There was just one qualification—a successful "practice run" on the 22,500-foot Ama Dablam, seven miles south of Everest.

That's how Eric found himself in the Himalayas in April 2000, pinned in a tent with Weihenmayer for six days, waiting for a storm to pass. The deteriorating weather finally forced the team to abandon its summit hopes.

Eric descended Ama Dablam with three teammates and two Sherpas. After enduring a long session of down climbing and rappels through freezing wind and snow, Eric was exhausted and ready to crawl into his sleeping bag in his tent at camp 1. With the tents in sight, he unclipped from the end of the fixed rope and started the short but still dangerous descent down the narrow, steep path to camp. Below the path was a nearly vertical drop of more than six hundred feet.

All it took was one wrong step. The three-foot rock beneath his boot began to slide. Eric's feet went out from under him. He fell on the rock and felt himself and the rock slipping.

He grabbed for the edge of the path, but his heavy gloves found no traction.

He was going down.

He bounced off the slope and was airborne for a few feet, and then he slammed against the mountain again, his helmeted head cracking against rock, before being flung once more into space.

His thoughts distilled to single-word sentences: *Help! Stop!*

And then he wasn't falling. His feet slid against a protrusion on the mountain and held there. With his stomach against the face, Eric slowly turned his head and looked down.

He was amazed by what he saw. He was "standing" on a ledge about three feet long and extending two feet out of the slope. It was the only barrier on the face. Below it was another sheer drop of nearly five hundred feet.

Eric did a quick self-check. His elbow hurt and his climbing outfit was shredded, but he hadn't broken any bones. It was as if God had said, "No, Eric, not today."

His teammates lowered a rope, and Eric climbed back to camp. His ordeal wasn't over, however. That night, because of the shock of the fall, he developed high-altitude pulmonary edema. His lungs filled with fluid. His oxygen saturation rate—a normal level is 97 to 99 percent—dropped to 45 percent. The expedition doctor told Eric they needed to get him off the mountain quickly. He didn't mention that with that much fluid in his lungs, Eric should already be dead.

A snowstorm, the altitude, and the steep slope made a helicopter rescue impossible. Eric was forced to rappel from camp 1 and then walk with the doctor to base camp, where a helicopter flew him to a hospital.

It was a trying time. As he attempted to recover, Eric caught pneumonia. The Everest expedition was only eight months away. He found himself praying for signs that he should stay home.

Eric realized he was afraid.

There was justification for his fear. People who develop high-altitude pulmonary edema once are more likely to suffer from it again. Eric wondered if his teammates would see him as bad luck or someone who had to be watched. He didn't want to put his family through more trauma after they'd just recovered from his fall on Ama Dablam.

He also considered warnings emerging from the climbing community. Some felt that Weihenmayer was putting his life, as well as the lives of his teammates, at unwarranted risk. If Weihenmayer didn't reach the summit or if anything went wrong, people would see the expedition as a failure. Eric didn't want to let his friend down.

As Eric weighed his decision, he was rocked by a heartbreaking loss. His prayer partner, climbing buddy, and best friend, a free spirit named Joseph, went snowboarding alone into backcountry near Vail. When he didn't show up for work the next day, Eric and a team of ski patrol friends mounted a search. They found Joseph at the bottom of a cliff, upside down in the snow. He'd suffocated.

Eric knew Joseph wanted him to go to Everest. *I can't just quit*, he thought. *He'd be so mad at me if I did.*

A Boulder doctor cleared Eric to go. His teammates encouraged him to come back. The final hurdle was Weihenmayer himself. Eric asked what he thought he should do.

"People have always made judgments on what I can and can't do," Weihenmayer said. "I'm not about to do the same thing to you. You've got to decide for yourself."

As Eric thought about it, he realized that the Everest expedition was about more than his own struggle. It had the potential to open new horizons for the blind and anyone held back by what seemed an insurmountable obstacle. He wanted to be part of that. He also sensed the Lord's direction through Bible verses such as Joshua 1:9: "Be strong and courageous . . . for the LORD your God will be with you wherever you go."

"I'm not sure if I'm strong enough to get you to the top or get myself to the top," he told Weihenmayer a few days later, "but I know I'm strong enough to help you get there."

On Everest in March and April 2001, Eric has plenty of opportunities to wonder if he's made the right decision. Weihenmayer's first trip through the treacherous Himalayan glacier known as the Khumbu Icefall takes thirteen intense hours instead of the scheduled seven, putting the goal of a summit in serious doubt. Then there is the issue with Eric's heart rate, followed by the rock-dodging adventure on the Lhotse face.

But Weihenmayer and Eric both persevere. As the climbers acclimatize to the altitude, repeatedly moving up and down the mountain, Weihenmayer gradually improves his speed through the icefall to a much quicker five hours. Eric's health problems disappear, and he rejoins the rest of the team.

Finally, on May 24, after two years of preparation and weeks of climbing and waiting for the right weather on the mountain, Eric, Weihenmayer, and the rest of the team are at camp 4, ready for the summit push.

The mood is a combination of excitement, nervous anticipation, and bald fear. Even while sitting in a tent at twenty-six thousand feet, every breath is labored, and simple decisions require intense concentration. The climbers are in the Death Zone, a place where no human can expect to live for long. They're well aware that the day before, an Austrian climber clipped into the wrong rope at the Hillary Step and fell. It was a fatal mistake.

By radio, the team gets word that a Spanish climber is missing somewhere on the slopes above them. Some begin preparing to aid in the search. Eric is asked to pray. He does, silently, and encourages the others to do the same. Minutes later, the team receives the good news that the missing climber is found and everyone's okay.

At 9 p.m. that night, wearing a green down suit, backpack, oxygen tank, and goggles, Eric steps out of his tent onto the South Col. He's greeted by subzero temperatures and a punishing wind. Everest is in the jet stream, where the air can easily fly faster than one hundred miles per hour. It's time to move.

Every step is a struggle, but the climbers push forward. Eric is just behind Weihenmayer, focused on making sure his friend stays on route. When they reach the Southeast Ridge at 27,500 feet, they trudge into a storm marked by lightning and snow. It appears they'll have to turn around, until base camp radios a forecast: the storm will pass. Coated in two inches of snow, they decide to continue up.

At 8:30 in the morning, the climbers reach the South Summit, three hundred vertical feet from the peak but still two hours of climbing away. They must negotiate a knife-edge ridge more than six hundred feet long. On the left side is a seven-thousand-foot drop into Nepal. On the right is a ten-thousand-foot drop into Tibet.

Eric looks at the precarious ridge and shakes his head. *How are we going to get across this?* But Weihenmayer is already on his way. Eric isn't going to leave his friend now.

The weather is clearing when they attack the Hillary Step, the thirty-nine-foot rock face named after the first man to ascend the world's tallest peak. Eric is just behind Weihenmayer when his friend takes hold of a rope, one of several that stretch down from the top of the face. Some are new and secure; some have been here for multiple climbing seasons.

Eric remembers the fate of the Austrian. He tells Weihenmayer, "Hey, Erik, there are a bunch of ropes here. Don't grab just one. Grab 'em all."

Finally, far above the clouds and beneath a brilliant blue sky, Eric, Weihenmayer, and the rest of the team make the final steps up to the small platform that marks the roof of the world.

"Wooo!" Eric shouts.

"Erik, you did it, man! You showed 'em!" yells another teammate.

"I can't believe it," says Weihenmayer.

It's a joyful moment marked by backslaps and hugs. But Eric has one private duty to perform. He's been carrying a picture of Joseph against his chest throughout the summit push. Now he takes it out, intending to secure it under a rock at the summit.

The wind has other ideas. The photo is ripped from Eric's hands. It begins a flight into the seemingly endless airspace over Tibet, the birth of a new adventure. Startled at first, Eric quickly realizes that his friend would probably prefer it this way.

The team doesn't linger—they know how unforgiving this mountain can be to those who underestimate its power. Eric attaches the bell to his pack and prepares to lead Weihenmayer back into the world of mortals. He pauses one last time to speak to the Source of even greater power.

Thank you, Lord, for Joseph's and Erik's friendship, and for allowing us to make it this far. Please help us to get down safely.

Feeling stronger than ever, Eric steps off the summit and toward his next challenge.

Would You? Could You?

(Share your answers if you're reading in a group)

Before the Weihenmayer expedition, many people questioned the idea of a blind man attempting to summit Everest. Climber and author Jon Krakauer wrote to Weihenmayer, "I am not at all enthusiastic about your trip to Everest next spring . . . I don't think you can get to the top of that particular hill without subjecting yourself to horrendous risk, the same horrendous risk all Everest climbers face, and then some." Ed Viesturs, one of America's most prolific climbers, said in an interview, "I support his going. But I wouldn't want to take him up there myself . . . They'll have to be helping him, watching out for him every step of the way." That skepticism continued on the mountain itself. One climber planned to stay close to the expedition so he could "get the first picture of the dead blind guy." Even at camp 4, just before the final summit push, another climber stuck his head into one of the team's tents and, without realizing Weihenmayer was there, said, "You're gonna have a heck of a time getting that blind guy up there."

Weihenmayer's team was far from typical, however. Eric and the others were more than just experienced climbers. They were friends who had climbed with Weihenmayer many times before. As Eric says, "We are the experts on ourselves, and as a team we trusted each other. We might let the mountain turn us back, but we weren't going to let the 'experts' stop us."

It takes fortitude and courage to push forward in the face of pessimism and doubt. How willing are you to take big risks when everyone around you says, "No way"?

- If you had the technical ability, *would you*, like Eric Alexander, accept an invitation to help a blind friend summit Everest? Why or why not? If you couldn't see, *would you* take on a challenge like Everest?

- Do you agree or disagree with Krakauer's comments—was the risk acceptable or too high? Why? Would your opinion be any different if someone on the expedition had been hurt or killed?

- Eric survived brushes with death on both Ama Dablam and Everest. He attributes the team's success and his survival to God's grace, saying, "There were too many close calls. How did nineteen of us (an Everest record for one expedition) make the summit? How did I come back without any strength or training?" Is Eric brave or foolhardy? How about Erik Weihenmayer? Do you think God was looking out for them?

- Read Psalm 121, which says, "The LORD will keep you from all harm" (v. 7). Sometimes bad things *do* happen to us, so what does this mean?
- How important was friendship and teamwork to this expedition? How important is it in your life?
- Eric teaches disabled skiers and works with an organization that educates and encourages youth with disabilities in the outdoors. What are you doing to help people overcome obstacles in their lives?
- Do you usually abide by the advice of the "experts" in your life? When have you gone against their counsel? How did that turn out? What does it mean to be an "expert on yourself"?

Reporting In

Is anyone's "expert" opinion holding you back from pursuing God's calling on your life? Ask the Lord whether your expert's words are wise or misguided advice.

Hitting the Trail

(This is just for you)

Eric Alexander gives the credit for his courage on Everest to his standing with God. He knew he had a room reserved in heaven. "Ultimately, what made the climb possible for me was the knowledge that my soul was secure with him," Eric says. "I knew that if I died, that wouldn't be the worst thing that could happen to me. My teammates didn't have that security and confidence, and it showed."

It makes sense. It's easier to risk your life for a worthy cause if you're certain you're destined for a better, eternal life. So . . . how certain are you?

- Whether you've given your heart to Jesus Christ or not, write down what you believe would happen to your soul if you died today. What is the foundation for your belief? How sure are you—60 percent? Ninety percent? What would it take to make you absolutely certain?

_____

_____

_____

- Maybe you're a believer, but your faith comes and goes. Read Matthew 14:29–31 and John 20:25. The faith of the disciples, who witnessed the physical presence of Jesus, wavered as well. Does this mean it's okay for us to doubt our faith? What causes you to doubt? How do you respond to 2 Corinthians 5:7?

_____

_____

_____

- What draws you closer to the presence of God? A sunrise? Time alone reading Scripture? A demanding climb on a dangerous mountain? Make a list of the environments and activities that lead you deeper in your faith journey. Write down how it might be possible for you to spend more time seeking the Lord and a certain faith.

_____

_____

_____

New Territory

(For those who want to explore further)

Watch *Farther Than the Eye Can See*, a documentary about the Weihenmayer team's Everest expedition directed by Michael Brown, and read *Touch the Top of the World*, Weihenmayer's biography through 2001.

- How willing are you to take on the responsibility for someone else's life, as Eric Alexander and the rest of his teammates did on Everest?
- At the end of his book, Weihenmayer says life would be easier if he could see, but he's not sure it would be more exciting or satisfying. How can risk and challenge make life more rewarding?

2

Death and Birth in Blue John Canyon

When we find inspiration, we need to take action
. . . even if it means making a hard choice or cutting out something and leaving it in your past.

Aron Ralston

Saturday, April 26, 2003, 2:51 p.m.
Blue John Canyon, Utah

Twenty-seven-year-old Aron Ralston stands in a slot canyon and weighs the dilemma before him. To continue down the canyon, he must go over a boulder the size of a bus tire that's wedged between the walls at his feet, then drop twelve feet to the canyon floor. Beyond the boulder, the walls rise sixty feet to the canyon rim and taper to just three feet wide. It's a narrow, open-roofed tunnel carved in stone.

Aron kicks at the boulder; it seems secure enough to hang from. He squats, puts his weight onto the boulder, turns to face the direction he just came from, and slides over the boulder so he's dangling, arms extended, from its front.

Unexpectedly, the boulder shifts.

Aron knows this is bad news. He lets go and drops to the rocks below.

He looks up. The boulder is falling on top of him. He throws his hands up to protect himself. The boulder bashes Aron's left hand against the south wall, then ricochets and smashes down on his right hand, ripping it down the wall for a foot before coming to rest between both walls, pinning Aron's right hand against the north wall.

The pain is excruciating. Aron pulls hard three times at his arm. He pushes with all his might on the boulder.

Nothing happens.

He's alone, hidden in a remote canyon in southeast Utah, and he's stuck.

---

6 p.m.

Aron scratches at the boulder, first with the file end and then with the knife blade of his multiuse tool. His progress is pitifully slow. The boulder has the same appearance as the dark material that formed the canyon lip. His blade is rapidly losing its sharpness. *This chock stone*, Aron thinks, *is the hardest thing here.*

Aron is an experienced outdoorsman. He's trained in search and rescue. He's just spent the winter climbing some of Colorado's highest and toughest peaks. He knows how to work out problems under pressure. He's a graduate of Carnegie Mellon, for heaven's sake. But none of his training and experiences has prepared him for what he faces now.

He'd planned only for a bike ride and day hike through the canyons. The bike is hidden far back on the trail behind some bushes. His resources now are a CD player, a video camera, a headlamp, a rock-climbing harness and rappelling gear, two small burritos, and twenty-two ounces of water. Those and his brain are all he's got.

What makes matters worse is that Aron has committed a cardinal sin for outdoor adventurers. Because he wanted to keep his options open, he left no detailed description of his plans. The only hint he gave his roommates in Aspen, Colorado, was a single word: Utah.

Unless he finds a way to get out of here, he'll miss the party at his home on Monday night. He'll miss the first day he's due back at his job at Ute Mountaineering on Tuesday. Eventually, people will begin searching. But it will be too late. With so little water, Aron figures he'll last until Monday or Tuesday morning at best.

"You're gonna have to cut your arm off," Aron says out loud.

"But I don't wanna cut my arm off!" He's arguing with himself.

"Aron, you're gonna have to cut your arm off."

Yet he knows he can't saw through his arm bones with his small, dull knife.

He scratches at the boulder some more.

Sunday, 1 p.m.

With his climbing gear, Aron's rigged a pulley system around the boulder in an attempt to move it. But the system is too weak. No matter how hard he tries, the boulder won't budge. It must weigh two hundred pounds, maybe more.

Suddenly, Aron hears the echo of voices in the canyon.

Could it be? It's the right time of day—a group would get to this part and be able to return out to the West Fork or to Horseshoe Trailhead in daylight.

"Help!" he shouts. "Helllp!"

Aron's heart pounds, but there is no other sound. Then he hears the echo again. This time, Aron recognizes what it really is—a kangaroo rat scratching in its nest above the boulder.

With few other options, Aron again considers amputation. He can fashion a tourniquet from materials at hand. He wonders, assuming he figures out a way to cut through his bones, if he has the courage to go through with it.

Aron presses the knife blade of his multitool against his arm near the wrist. He can see tendons and veins beneath the skin. He feels nauseous.

What are you doing, Aron? Get that knife away from your wrist! What are you trying to do, kill yourself? That's suicide! I don't care how good a tourniquet you have, you've got too many arteries in your arm to stop them all. You'll bleed out.

The idea of slashing his wrists to end the ordeal flashes through Aron's mind.

"I . . . hate . . . this!"

Sunday evening

Aron rests his left hand on the boulder and closes his eyes.

"God, I am praying to you for guidance," he says. "I'm trapped here in Blue John Canyon—you probably know that—and I don't know what I am supposed to do. I've tried everything I can think of. I need some new ideas. Or if I need to try something again—lifting the boulder, amputating my arm—please show me a sign."

Aron waits. There's no discernible answer.

Monday, 3 p.m.

Aron pulls out his video camera. He's already recorded an explanation of the accident. Now it's time to leave more thoughts.

"One of the things I'm learning here is that I didn't enjoy the people's company that I was with enough, or as much as I should have," he says. "A lot of really good people have spent a lot of time with me. Very often I would tend to ignore or diminish their presence in seeking the essence of the experience. All that's to say, I'm figuring some things out . . .

"I'm doing what I can, but this sucks. It's really bad. This is one of the worst ways to go. Knowing what's going to happen, but it still being three or four days out."

He pauses.

"I did want to say, on the logistical side of things, I have some American Express insurance that should cover costs of the recovery operation when that does happen . . ."

Tuesday morning

Aron is recording again.

"This next part may not be for all viewers at home," he says to the camera. "It's a little after eight. At precisely eight o'clock I took my last sip of clean water . . . and . . . hide your eyes, Mom . . ."

He swivels the camera and reveals a bloody wound in his right forearm.

"I made an attempt—a short career in surgery, as it turned out. Those knives are just not anywhere close to the task. I've got about an inch-wide gash in my arm that goes about a half-inch deep. I cut down through the skin and the fatty tissue, and through some of the muscle. I think I cut a tendon, but I'm not sure. I tried, anyway. It really just didn't go well. The tourniquet is relaxed at this point. Which actually is a little bothersome, considering I'm not bleeding that bad, barely at all. It's so weird. You'd expect to definitely see more pulsing and bleeding, but oh well."

Aron stops the tape. He can't move the chock stone. He can't cut through his arm bones. Now he's really depressed.

He wonders which threat will actually be the one to finish him off—dehydration, hypothermia, a flash flood, toxins from his dying hand, or infection from the new wound in his arm.

1:30 p.m.
Aron is out of options. He's waiting for death.
He decides it's time for another prayer.
"God, it's Aron again. I still need your help. It's getting bad here. I'm out of water and food. I know I'm going to die soon, but I want to go naturally. I've decided that regardless of what I might go through, I don't want to take my own life. It occurred to me that I could, but that's not the way I want to go. As it is, I don't figure I'll live another day—it's been three days already—I don't figure I'll see Wednesday noon. But please, God, grant me the steadfastness not to do anything against my being."
He's resolved to hang on until the bitter end.

Wednesday, 4 a.m.
Aron has rigged a kind of chair from his climbing gear, but if he sits in it for more than a few minutes it cuts off the circulation in his legs. Otherwise, he stands. He can't sleep. He's been awake since Friday night.
He does, however, enter into a series of trances. In front of the boulder, he sees a man in a white robe motion for him to follow. Aron presses on the sandstone wall, and it swings open like a gate. He steps into a living room filled with friends at a dinner party. He can see them, and they can see him, but they can't interact physically.
What's going on? he thinks. *What's happening to me here? Am I inside my head? Am I dreaming? How can that be, if I'm not sleeping? But how is this possible if it's not a dream?*

34

Aron is racked by spasms of cold. He's back in the canyon, his hand still trapped by the boulder. The night grinds on. In each new vision, he's no longer aware of cold or pain or hunger or thirst. But each trance ends with convulsions and the reality of the canyon.

---

11 p.m.

Aron is freezing. Even the slightest breeze leaves him shivering uncontrollably.

He begins carving on the sandstone wall above his left shoulder. When he's done, the rock reveals his final message to the world: ARON. OCT 75. APR 03. RIP.

Thursday, 10:30 a.m.

Inexplicably, Aron is still alive, though barely. He's been drinking his own urine, and it's eroding the inside of his mouth. His lips are horribly chapped. He's still wearing his contact lenses; every blink hurts. He weighed about 175 pounds on Saturday. Who knows what he weighs now?

He's beyond exhaustion, beyond everything. Waiting for the inevitable is the worst part of all.

Yesterday, he picked up a rock and pounded at the boulder, with small effect. He reaches again for the rock. His left hand is already raw from yesterday's effort. Now each blow brings on new agony.

Finally, Aron stops and puts the rock down. Dirt and bits of sandstone cover his right arm. With his multitool knife, he brushes some off. He accidentally nicks himself, exposing a section of decomposed flesh. He understands that his right hand is already dead.

Curious explorer to the end, he punctures the skin on his right thumb. It hisses; a stench rises to his nose.

Suddenly, Aron has had it. This dying appendage is no longer part of him. It's poison. It's garbage. He hates it. *Throw it away, Aron. Be rid of it.*

The amazing cool he's maintained so carefully for the last five days is finally used up. He's enraged. He's screaming. He yanks again and again with his right arm, smashing his fading body against the walls of his familiar trap. His contortions force his right arm to bend at a strange angle.

Aron stops. His fury has provided an epiphany. If he applies enough force, he can bend his arm so far that the bones will break.

That's it!

There is no analysis or reflection. Aron immediately crouches as low as he can beneath the boulder, putting tension on his forearm, pushing, pushing harder still.

A popping sound from his arm echoes up the canyon walls.

Seconds later, Aron repeats his violent dance with the boulder and produces a second popping noise. He's successfully broken the radius and ulna bones in his forearm. He's excited and sweating hard. He's also in pain, but he's not thinking about that. After days of forced immobility, he's focused only on action.

Clutching his multitool, Aron tackles his next grisly task—separating his body from his decaying wrist and hand. After nearly an hour of twisting and cutting, with a break to apply his makeshift tourniquet, he makes the final slice.

Aron is overwhelmed by an ecstasy he's never known. It is a second birth.

I AM FREE!

3:00 p.m.

Despite the tourniquet and layers of clothes wrapped to make a bandage, blood is dripping steadily from Aron's right arm. He's rappelled down six stories to a waterhole in Blue John Canyon and hiked six miles through punishing heat to this point in Horseshoe Canyon. He has only two miles to go to reach the trailhead where he parked his truck five days ago, but the hike includes a steep rise at the end, and his energy is nearly gone. The outcome of his ordeal is still very much in doubt.

Aron follows a left turn on the trail. Seventy yards ahead is a sight so unbelievable that he wonders if it's real. Three people, two adults and a child, are on the trail. They are walking away.

Twice, Aron tries to shout, but he can't get any words out of his parched throat. Then comes a feeble sound, followed by a stronger one: "Help! HELP!"

The trio stops and turns around. Then they start running in his direction.

Aron nearly begins to cry. He's no longer alone.

He's going to live.

Would You? Could You?

(Share your answers if you're reading in a group)

Aron Ralston has been praised and criticized for his actions during the last days of April 2003. Many consider him a hero and an inspiration. One woman sent him a letter, saying, "I had promised myself that I would end my life if things had not gotten better one year after my husband's death. I know now that suicide is not the answer. You inspire me to stay strong, remain brave, and fight for life." Others point to his narrow escapes on previous adventures and his failure to leave word of his plans and conclude that he is foolish. One book reviewer said, "Aron Ralston has a death wish."

Whatever your take on Aron Ralston, it appears that when he faced the greatest challenge of his life, he found the courage and motivation to meet it. Despite truly desperate circumstances, he kept his composure and endured until a solution presented itself—and then had the fortitude to follow through on his opportunity to escape.

Life is a precious gift. How much does yours mean to you?

- *Would you* cut off a limb to save your life? If you were stuck in Aron Ralston's shoes, *could you* work out the necessary steps to stay alive and rescue yourself?
- How did Aron demonstrate his courage most—by refusing to panic, by rejecting thoughts of suicide, or by breaking his forearm bones and cutting off his hand?
- Aron has named love as the source of his courage, saying, "We're tapping into that source of strength and courage when we feel love, and we do it for our families and our friends and hopefully for the world at large. Those opportunities are out there all the time, and hopefully we're doing it for that instead of just our own egos." Is love the source of everyone's courage? If God is love (1 John 4:8), is this another way of saying that God is the source of our courage?
- After the accident, Aron continued to take risks. He completed his goal of solo-climbing the fourteen-thousand-foot peaks of Colorado. Yet he sounds changed by his encounter in the canyon, saying, "I still do like adventures. But it's different. It's not coming from an esteem-building, need-fulfillment place, like my life won't amount to something if I'm not the first person to make some major accomplishment." What do you think he means? How would such an experience change you?
- Aron has written that if he could travel back in time to Blue John Canyon in 2003, he would still go through it all again. Why might he feel this way?
- Aron's escape happened at just the right time. If he'd left a day or two earlier, he might easily have bled to death while hiking back in a deserted canyon. If he'd waited another day for rescuers to find him, he likely would have

died from dehydration. Was it coincidence that caused him to find a solution at just the right moment?

Reporting In

Are you feeling trapped in any area of your life? Is there a hard choice you need to make to escape? Pray about it with the Lord.

Hitting the Trail

(This is just for you)

Before the accident, Aron Ralston had quit his job as an engineer and moved to Aspen to pursue outdoor adventures. Sonja Ralston Elder, Aron's sister, said, "What happened to him has vindicated this choice about doing what you love and not being defined by other people's expectations."

Most of us live, often unconsciously, with the expectations of others in our heads—those of our friends, parents, co-workers, and society in general. Who is defining your life?

- Make a list of the activities you're involved in, whether they are jobs, hobbies, volunteer work, or something else. Why do you participate in each?

  _____

  _____

  _____

- How would your list change if you paid no attention to the expectations of others?

  _____

  _____

  _____

- How important is it to weigh the opinions of others before we act, especially if the "other" is a friend, parent, sibling, or anyone who might be affected by what we do? Where does God fit into this equation? Read John 14:23–24 and record your response here.

_____

_____

_____

New Territory

(For those who want to explore further)

Read *Desert Solitaire*, Edward Abbey's reflections on a season as a park ranger near Moab, Utah, and *Into the Wild*, Jon Krakauer's account of the travels and death of young Chris McCandless in the Alaskan wilderness.

- What do we have to gain from spending time alone in the desert or wilderness?
- In what ways can you relate to Aron Ralston, Edward Abbey, and Chris McCandless? In what ways are you entirely different?

3

Back on Board

Be strong and courageous . . . for the LORD your God goes with you; he will never leave you nor forsake you.

Deuteronomy 31:6

A blustery wind and the sound of waves crashing onto the sand greet blonde-haired, thirteen-year-old Bethany Hamilton as she gets out of the van. A short walk down the trail and a quick inspection of the beach confirm everyone's hopes—it's a great spot for surfing.

Originally, Bethany had planned only to watch. She was going to just sit in the sand while her friends rode their boards. But the water, the waves, and the perfect conditions are too tempting. After all, her dream has been to become a professional surfer. She's already been successful as an amateur on the National Scholastic Surfing Association (NSSA) circuit and even has a sponsor. She has to try it.

She has to know, after everything that's happened, if she can still surf.

It was just a month ago that Bethany's life changed forever. On Halloween morning 2003, Bethany was doing what she loved most, what she'd been doing every chance she had since she'd first tried surfing at the age of seven. She and her best friend, Alana Blanchard, along with Alana's brother, Byron, and dad, Holt, were surfing at Tunnels, a beach on the north shore of the Hawaiian island of Kauai. The waves weren't spectacular, but that didn't matter. Bethany didn't want to be anywhere else.

After about half an hour in the water, Holt and Byron were on their boards and farthest from the beach. Alana trailed behind them in the water, and Bethany was about fifteen feet behind her friend, a quarter mile from shore. Bethany was lying on her stomach on her red, white, and blue surfboard, looking out to sea. Her right arm rested on the nose of her board. Her left arm, the one with a shiny, light blue watch, dangled in the crystal clear water.

I hope the surf picks up soon, Bethany thought.

There was no warning, no sound or change in the pattern of the calm water. Just a sudden, unexpected presence at her left—something large and gray.

At the same instant Bethany registered the presence, she felt pressure on her arm, a jiggling, and a tug.

By the time she could fully turn her head to look at the blur of movement, the shape was gone. The water was turning bright red. There was a huge crescent-shaped hole in the surfboard. And all that remained of what should have been Bethany's left arm was a three- or four-inch stub.

Bethany's voice was loud yet surprisingly under control: "I just got attacked by a shark!" She began paddling toward shore.

Get to the beach, she thought. *Get to the beach.*

A minute later, Holt and Byron appeared at Bethany's side. "I can't believe that this happened," Bethany said.

Holt's face was white, his eyes wide, as he took in the sight of Bethany's bleeding stump and shredded board. "Oh my gosh!" he said. He began pushing the tail of Bethany's board to move her faster.

Please, God, help me, she prayed. *God, let me get to the beach.*

Fear began to enter Bethany's mind. *I could die.* She pushed the negative thoughts aside. *I'm in God's hands.*

At a shallow point, Holt stood up, took off his gray rash guard, and wrapped it tight around the stub of Bethany's arm. It was a makeshift tourniquet.

Fifteen minutes after the attack, Bethany, Holt, and Alana reached shore. Byron had already paddled ahead to call 911.

Holt lifted Bethany off her board and onto the sand. Bethany blacked out for a time. Alana ran for help and located a vacationing paramedic named Paul Wheeler. When someone produced a first-aid kit, Wheeler slipped on gloves and explored Bethany's wound with his fingers. Then he took her pulse.

Wheeler shook his head. "She's lost a lot of blood," he said in a low voice.

An ambulance finally arrived. As they pulled out of the parking lot with Bethany inside, a paramedic whispered in her ear, "God will never leave you or forsake you."

At that moment, at Wilcox Memorial Hospital, Bethany's father was on an operating table preparing for knee surgery. An emergency room nurse interrupted before the procedure could start. "Just a heads-up, Dr. Rovinsky," she said. "There's a thirteen-year-old girl coming—a shark attack victim. We are going to need this room right away."

Something in Tom Hamilton's heart told him the girl was either Alana or his daughter. The doctor left to investigate and returned a few minutes later. There were tears in his eyes.

"Tom, it's Bethany," he said. "She's in stable condition. That's all I know, I don't have any other information. Tom, I'm going to have to roll you out. Bethany's coming in here."

Not long after, Bethany lay in the same room while the doctor prepared for the unexpected surgery on a different member of the Hamilton family. "Do you want anything?" a nurse asked Bethany.

"Just to go to sleep," she said.

"Okay, Bethany," the nurse said. "Close your eyes and sleep."

Later that day, after the surgery and after the anesthesia had worn off, an exhausted young teen began dealing with the new reality of her life. Bethany told her dad, "I want to be the best surf photographer in the world." It was her way of saying that she understood her surfing dreams had ended.

By the next day, however, Bethany was already starting to feel a trickle of hope. So many people were saying positive things, cheering her up. Her doctor said that the list of things she could no longer do would be short. Was it possible her dream could stay off that list—that she could still surf competitively?

When she thought about going back into the ocean, Bethany didn't feel any deep fear of another shark attack. She was more scared of having to let go of her passion.

Now, just a few weeks after the attack, Bethany is standing on a beach at Kilauea, ready to face her fears and discover her future. She's selected her nine-foot board, which is easier to catch and maneuver than shorter ones. "You can do it," she says to herself on the beach. "You can paddle and get up with one arm."

A voice inside her head yells a rebuttal: *Forget it. You're going to fail.*

Bethany tries to ignore the voice and steps into the water.

She's far from alone at this critical moment. Her brother Noah is swimming out with Bethany, holding a video camera. Her dad is there too, taking time off work, shouting, "Go, girl!" Alana and many other friends are also on the beach.

As they have so many times before, Bethany and Alana walk deeper into the refreshing Hawaiian surf. Bethany revels in the warmth of the water and the taste of salt on her lips. It's like being home again.

She decides to begin by riding some "soup" (rolling white water). It's different paddling with just one arm; Bethany feels like a beginner. When the wave starts to pick her up, Bethany places her right hand in the middle of the board and tries to get on her feet.

It doesn't work.

A minute later, she tries a second time. Again, no luck.

Bethany's getting discouraged. She thought it would be easier than this. She can't even stand up.

"Bethany, try it one more time," Tom Hamilton shouts from the water. "This one will be it!"

Another wave tumbles in. Bethany positions her hand on her board and pushes up. She finds her balance. She's standing! She's surfing!

Joy and a sense of gratitude well up inside Bethany. With that one wave, all the doubts vanish. Tears begin running down her face, mixing with the ocean water. Everyone in the water and on the beach cheers.

Now Bethany believes anything is possible.

That first day back in the water marks the beginning of an impressive return to competitive surfing for Bethany. She finds ways to compensate for the loss of her arm and refines her technique. The next year, she is presented with a special courage award at the Teen Choice Awards sponsored by FOX and wins a Best Comeback ESPY award from ESPN. More important to Bethany, in 2005 she wins an NSSA amateur national championship.

Three years later, Bethany starts competing full-time on the Association of Surfing Professionals (ASP) World Qualifying

Series. She's achieved her dream—she is a professional, at this writing just one step away from qualifying for the pinnacle of the sport, the ASP World Tour. In Bethany's first competition against many of the world's best surfers, she finishes third.

At five feet ten inches, Bethany has turned into a statuesque, even imposing, figure on a surfboard. She also appears fearless in the water.

"She's really aggressive," says one competitor. "Bethany catches really big waves. Like, gnarly waves."

She's not always as fearless as she seems. She admits that sometimes her heart pounds when she's in the ocean and sees a shadow in the water.

Bethany sometimes asks herself why the shark attack happened at all. There was no record of a shark ever attacking a human on Kauai's north coast. But when Bethany asks, "Why me?" it isn't usually a negative question. She's not asking, "Why did this horrible thing have to happen to me?" For Bethany, it's more about wondering, "Why did God choose me and what does he have in mind for me?"

Some of that question may have already been answered for Bethany. On the day of the attack, a family friend said that God had given her a message from the Bible for the Hamilton family: " 'For I know the plans I have for you,' declares the LORD, 'plans to prosper you and not to harm you, plans to give you hope and a future' " (Jer. 29:11).

Despite her natural shyness, Bethany has taken advantage of her unplanned celebrity to tell her story to the world through interviews, a book, and a documentary, lifting the spirits of millions through her courage. She's also used the opportunity to explain her faith in Jesus Christ. She has written, "I don't really want people looking to me for inspiration. I just want to be a sign along the way that points toward heaven."

For Bethany, the sign pointing to her future is as bright as a Hawaiian sunrise and as inviting as her beloved Pacific surf.

Would You? Could You?

(Share your answers if you're reading in a group)

David Rovinsky, the doctor who first performed surgery on Bethany Hamilton after she was attacked by a fourteen-foot tiger shark, described her as "cool as a cucumber" at the hospital. That coolness may have saved her life. Bethany lost nearly half of her blood volume; it would have been more if she hadn't stayed calm in the minutes after losing her arm. Her heartbeat stayed slow enough to prevent the severed artery from rapidly bleeding out. She understood she had to fight off the surging feelings of fear and panic. That skill, whether innate or acquired, brands Bethany a survivor.

Laurence Gonzales, in his book *Deep Survival: Who Lives, Who Dies, and Why*, writes: "It is not a lack of fear that separates elite performers from the rest of us. They're afraid, too, but they're not overwhelmed by it. They manage fear. They use it to focus on taking correct action. Mike Tyson's trainer, Cus D'Amato, said, 'Fear is like fire. It can cook for you. It can heat your house. Or it can burn you down.'"

So what's your "cucumber" rating? If the tiger sharks circling in your life suddenly attack, is your reaction closer to ice, or are you about as cool as a puddle of melted butter? The answer may mean the difference between becoming a survivor or just another victim.

- How about it—if you were in the ocean on your board and your arm had just disappeared into the gaping jaws of a sea monster, *could you* keep it together enough to stem the blood loss and paddle to shore?
- What do you think is the source of Bethany's courage and coolness? Was she born with it? Did she develop it by riding killer waves and challenging herself in surf competitions?
- Read the account of Jesus and Peter walking on water in Matthew 14:22–36. Does this imply a link between

courage and faith? Was faith a factor in Bethany's courage? Is it in yours? Do people of genuine faith have an advantage in crisis situations?

- Courage can take many forms. Bethany showed hers when she returned to the water and surfing. *Would you* be back in the ocean less than a month after a shark had ripped your arm off? *Could you* overcome a devastating loss to renew your passion?

- What about Bethany's willingness, despite her natural shyness, to talk about her love for Jesus in print interviews and on national television—is this also a form of courage? How is it the same as or different from her coolheaded response after the attack and her return to surfing?

- Have you ever made fear work for you in the way Mike Tyson's trainer described? Is there such a thing as good fear? What kind of fear was Jesus talking about when he said, "Do not be afraid of those who kill the body but cannot kill the soul. Rather, be afraid of the One who can destroy both soul and body in hell" (Matt. 10:28)?

Reporting In

Is the Lord calling you to act with greater courage in any area of your life? Take time now to talk with him about it.

Hitting the Trail

(This is just for you)

Not everyone is a world-class surfer or the victim of a shark attack, but we can all find ways to test ourselves and measure or develop our courage. And like Bethany Hamilton, aren't we most useful to God when we are ready to act with strength and courage on his behalf? Maybe it's not coincidence that you're reading this story today. Maybe the Lord is encouraging you to move boldly into the purpose he's designed just for you.

- Make a list of your greatest fears. What does this say about your courage? What does it say about your faith?

  _____

  _____

  _____

- Do you think you could take steps to decrease these fears and increase your courage? What would have to change in your life to make that happen? Is prayer and time in the Word part of the equation? Write down your thoughts here.

  _____

  _____

  _____

- Imagine how God might use you if you had more courage, whether that would involve making friends with someone you barely know, ending a relationship, leaving a party where people are drinking or doing drugs, speaking up in class about your faith, or doing something else. Write down what that might look like. Ask the Lord if this is part of his plan for you—and if so, what you should do next.

  _____

  _____

  _____

New Territory

(For those who want to explore further)

Watch *Heart of a Soul Surfer*, the documentary about Bethany Hamilton, and check out the Discovery Channel's internet shark guide at http://dsc.discovery.com/sharks/.

- What do you admire most about Bethany's life since the shark attack?

  _____

  _____

  _____

- How has your opinion changed, if at all, on the connection between courage and faith?

  _____

  _____

  _____

4

Not Without a Fight

Whoever said anybody has a right to give up?
Marian Wright Edelman

For seventeen-year-old Jacque Marris, a cheerleader at Highland High School in Palmdale, California, the last day of July 2002 begins as just another carefree summer evening. She has no inkling it will mark the most terrifying experience of her life.

It is a Wednesday night. Jacque and a friend, nineteen-year-old Frank Melero, have driven in Melero's truck to Quartz Hill, a teen hangout overlooking Antelope Valley, about an hour north of Los Angeles. They haven't seen each other in a while and want to catch up. On the way up the hill, they passed a white Ford Bronco and a Saturn parked next to it. Now, at the top, they are alone, listening to music, enjoying the view, and realizing it is nearly time to go—it's after midnight, almost to Jacque's curfew.

Suddenly, on Melero's side of the truck, a man appears out of the darkness. He's holding a gun.

"None of you look at me," the man says through the open window. "Both of you turn away."

Jacque's heart begins to pound. She and Melero turn. The man presses the gun against the side of Melero's head.

"Give me your money," the man says in a raspy voice. Melero hands over his wallet. The man also takes the keys to the truck.

He asks if Melero has rope or tape in the truck. Melero says no.

"Either you give me rope or tape or I'm going to hurt you both," the man says.

Melero remembers he has a nylon tie-down strap in the bed of the truck. The man uses it to tie Melero's arms to the steering wheel. Jacque, petrified, sits slumped over next to Melero, waiting and hoping the man will just go away.

Just as he finishes securing Melero, they all hear the sound of a vehicle approaching. It's a state water and power employee. The worker gets out of his truck, apparently to check on a gate.

"Don't move," the gunman whispers to Jacque and Melero, "or I'll kill you."

The state worker either doesn't see Melero's truck or doesn't notice what's happening. After a few minutes, he gets back into his own truck and drives away.

The gunman tries to bind Jacque next to Melero with the same nylon strap. Jacque feels for Melero's hands, tied to the steering wheel. "I'm really scared," she whispers.

"It's going to be all right," Melero answers. "God is with us."

The gunman can't get the strap to work. It isn't long enough. He curses and mumbles to himself. He makes Jacque get out of the truck and forces her to walk down the hill, leaving Melero and the truck behind.

Now she's terrified.

They reach the Bronco. The gunman finds duct tape in the back and uses it to tape Jacque's mouth and arms. They go back to check on Melero one more time, then return to the Bronco. Jacque is forced into the back. She's horrified to see someone's legs. She thinks it's a dead body.

The owner of the legs, however, is very much alive. She is sixteen-year-old Tamara Brooks, an honor student at Antelope Valley High School in Lancaster. The SUV they are in belongs to Tamara's friend Eric Brown. Just over an hour earlier, the gunman had bound Eric and Tamara with duct tape, then led Eric away.

The man turns on the Bronco's ignition and starts driving down the hill.

The girls are being kidnapped.

Jacque always sings when she's angry or in trouble. Now, fearing for both their lives, Jacque begins stroking Tamara's arms and legs and humming softly. Tamara later says it was like her mom was singing a lullaby to her.

The serenity is broken several minutes later. The man parks the Bronco in a remote area, climbs into the back, and sexually assaults both teens. Jacque can smell the alcohol on the man's breath. She can't believe this horrible nightmare is really happening.

The girls' kidnapper is thirty-seven-year-old Roy Dean Ratliff. He's been convicted of burglary and drug charges and is currently wanted for rape. He has two guns and ammunition.

After the assaults, Ratliff begins driving again. At one point, Jacque feels the vehicle roll to a stop on the highway shoulder. She sees and hears cars passing by, but she can't yell for help with the duct tape over her mouth.

Ratliff crawls into the passenger seat and then out the door, leaving it open a crack. This is Jacque's chance. Her arms and legs are tied, but only loosely. She figures she can jump out and flag someone down before the man catches her or drives off again.

There's just one problem with Jacque's plan—the girl tied up next to her.

I don't know what he'll do to her, if he'll hurt her more, Jacque thinks. *I can't leave her behind.*

A minute later, the kidnapper returns, slams the door, and revs the engine. The opportunity for escape is gone.

With the Bronco moving again, Jacque grabs Tamara's hand and traces letters into her palm: "Need a plan."

Tamara traces back a single word: "Knife." She knows her friend Eric keeps a bowie knife somewhere in the SUV. Moving silently, they search the back until they find the knife and a bottle that can also be used as a weapon.

Just past dawn, Ratliff drives onto a remote dirt road in the Mojave Desert. They are 130 miles from Quartz Hill. The kidnapper steps out of the Bronco and fires from both of his guns into the empty canyon.

He's going to kill us, Jacque thinks.

But before Ratliff can do anything else, his drinking apparently catches up with him. He sits down in the front seat, leaving the door slightly ajar, and falls asleep.

Jacque and Tamara work quickly to free themselves. They figure there is no way to get out of the Bronco without waking their kidnapper. He'd shoot them before they could run twenty yards.

Instead, they mouth the words to a different strategy: Jacque will stab Ratliff with the knife and Tamara will hit him with the bottle.

I'm so scared, Jacque thinks. *What if he wakes up? What if this doesn't work? Is God ever going to forgive us for this?*

Jacque grips the knife and hesitates. She isn't sure she can actually stab someone.

Then Ratliff's eyes flicker. He's waking up.

Jacque slashes at Ratliff's neck. Tamara smashes the bottle on his head.

Ratliff rolls to his left and falls partway out the still-open door. Together, Jacque and Tamara kick him the rest of the way out. They throw the knife and bottle at him, yank the door shut, and lock it.

That's when they realize their mistake. Ratliff still has the car key—and the guns.

"Open the door!" Ratliff yells. "Open the door or I'll kill you!"

"Don't you believe in Jesus?" Jacque yells back. "Isn't there going to be anyone who will be upset if you die?"

"No one cares about me!" Ratliff answers. He raises a pistol and fires a shot over the roof. The girls have no choice. They have to open the door.

Ratliff doesn't retaliate, at least not yet. Instead, his neck bleeding, he starts driving again and turns onto Highway 178. What he doesn't know is that Frank Melero has freed himself and used a cell phone to call his mother, who dialed 911. Authorities issue California's first AMBER Alert, a nationwide system designed to help recover abducted children. The AMBER program, which stands for America's Missing: Broadcast Emergency Response, was formed as a legacy for Amber Hagerman, a nine-year-old who was kidnapped while riding her bicycle in Arlington, Texas, and then brutally murdered. When a child is abducted, the news is quickly broadcast via television, radio, highway signs, the internet, and other resources.

On that summer morning in 2002, Milton Walters, a county employee, hears the reports about Jacque's and Tamara's kidnapping, which include a description of the stolen SUV. At about 11 a.m., while working on Highway 178, he's shocked to see a white Ford Bronco heading his way on the usually deserted highway. Walters stares at the driver, who gives him a strange smile and nod as he drives by.

Walters reaches for his cell phone.

In the Bronco, Jacque feels the SUV turn. The ride becomes bumpy. They're off the highway.

Jacque shudders. *He's going to kill us and dump our bodies in the brush.*

Suddenly, Jacque hears the whirring blades of a helicopter overhead. It gives her hope, but also a new surge of fear—Ratliff has promised to kill them if the police show up.

The Bronco begins moving faster. A few minutes later, it curves around a rock outcropping. Parked directly ahead is a Kern County patrol car.

Ratliff slams on the brakes. The Kern County deputy, already out of the car, draws his gun.

"Get your hands where I can see 'em!" the deputy yells.

"No . . . way!" Ratliff yells back. He whips the wheel and sends the Bronco to the left, where it sails over a small ridge into a dry creek bed. It lands hard on top of a large rock, nearly flipping over.

Ratliff guns the engine, but the Bronco doesn't move. He jumps into the backseat next to Jacque, his head on her shoulder, the pistol inches from her head.

He's gonna kill me right now, Jacque thinks.

"I have the girls!" Ratliff shouts. "You better not shoot or else they're gonna die!"

Jacque can see two deputies, both on foot with guns drawn, approaching the Bronco on the driver's side. In seconds, they're only six feet away.

Ratliff raises his gun toward one of the deputies.

The other deputy fires.

The air fills with the sounds of gunfire, exploding glass, and teenagers' screams. A few seconds later—after seventeen shots fired by the deputies and one by Ratliff—it's over. Ratliff is dead.

Crying and nearly hysterical, Jacque and Tamara scramble out of the Bronco. They embrace and then hug the deputies.

Jacque is overcome with relief. After twelve hours on the brink of death, she has her life back.

Today, Jacque says she has no regrets about staying with Tamara when she had the chance to escape. "I didn't know what he was gonna do to Tamara, if he would hurt her more than he already had," she says.

Jacque also believes she made the right choice to fight back against her abductor. "There was no way I wasn't going down without a fight because that would have been stupid of me," she says. "How can you not fight for your life?"

Because of the decisions Jacque Marris and Tamara Brooks made during those frightening hours in a Ford Bronco, both young women have a lifetime to answer that question.

Would You? Could You?

(Share your answers if you're reading in a group)

Does it get any worse than being held captive by an armed rapist? You've basically lost control of your circumstances—the bad guy with the gun gets to set the agenda.

Or does he? Not every expert agrees on the best response to an attempted abduction or sexual assault, and every situation is unique. But most authorities teach young kids to resist would-be kidnappers in any way they can—hit and scream, latch onto another person or object if possible, and "windmill" their arms so they're hard to grab. Similarly, many studies show that women who fight back during an assault have a better chance of avoiding rape (a swift kick to the groin can be very effective). Of course, you may need to think twice if the abductor holds a knife or gun. As in any emergency, keeping a clear head may be the best strategy of all.

Even though they were terrified, Jacque Marris and Tamara Brooks found the courage to fight back during their terrifying ordeal. Their actions may have kept them alive long enough to allow authorities to find and rescue the teens. Jacque made the additional brave choice to stay with Tamara when she might have had the chance to escape.

Someday, *you* could be the one confronting an armed gunman. What will you do?

- If you were in Jacque and Tamara's place, *would you* fight back against an armed abductor? *Would you* teach your children to resist?
- *Could you*, as Jacque did, attack a man with a knife if he was holding you captive?
- At a time of crisis, do you think you would be more courageous than normal or less so? Why?
- In his Sermon on the Mount, Jesus said, "You have heard that it was said, 'Eye for eye, and tooth for tooth.' But I tell you, Do not resist an evil person. If someone strikes you on the right cheek, turn to him the other also" (Matt. 5:38–39). Does turning the other cheek apply during a kidnapping, or is Jesus talking more about revenge here? Are there times when it is right to fight and other times when it is not? Which takes more courage? What is God's position on this?
- If you and a stranger were kidnapped victims and you saw a chance where you alone could escape, *would you* go or *would you* stay with the stranger? What would you base your decision on?
- In an interview after the incident, a family friend described Roy Ratliff as "a good man when he wasn't drinking." Frank Melero said that after hearing about Ratliff's death, he felt reassurance and at the same time sorrow at the loss of a life made by God. *Would you* feel any sorrow for Roy Ratliff if you were Frank Melero? How about if you were Jacque Marris or Tamara Brooks? *Could you* forgive a man who had kidnapped

or sexually assaulted you? How do you respond to these words of Jesus: "If you hold anything against anyone, forgive him, so that your Father in heaven may forgive you your sins" (Mark 11:25)?

Reporting In

At some point in the future, you may find yourself confronting your worst nightmare, a crisis that requires immediate life-or-death decisions. Ask God now to give you extra courage and wisdom when that moment arrives.

Hitting the Trail

(This is just for you)

Jacque Marris and Tamara Brooks had a face-to-face encounter with evil during the summer of 2002. Yet in our daily lives, each of us meets evil in various forms. Whether it's cruelty, lies, greed, emotional abuse, or any of a thousand other varieties—in others or in ourselves—we know it when we see it.

It sometimes takes courage to resist what you know is wrong. You're afraid of looking stupid. You fear you might fail. You think someone else who is better qualified will take care of it. But sometimes, ready or not, God is calling on *you* to take a stand.

- What evils or sins did you run across in the last week? How did you handle them? Would you say you were courageous in your actions?

_____

_____

_____

_____

- Scripture says, "Your enemy the devil prowls around like a roaring lion looking for someone to devour. Resist him, standing firm in the faith, because you know that your brothers throughout the world are undergoing the same kind of sufferings" (1 Peter 5:8–9). Make a list of the spiritual tools and weapons that allow someone to resist the enemy. How many do you possess? Which do you lack?

  _____

  _____

  _____

- Write down at least three Bible verses that deal with strength or courage (for examples, see Deut. 31:6; Ps. 27:1; and 2 Tim. 1:7). Choose one (or more) to memorize in the next week.

  _____

  _____

  _____

New Territory

(For those who want to explore further)

Read "Escape from Kashmir," Sebastian Junger's account of the kidnapping by terrorists of six foreign tourists and the subsequent escape of American John Childs.

- How were the circumstances and escape opportunities facing Jacque Marris and John Childs different? How were they the same?
- Do you believe John Childs made the right choice to run? What would you have done?

PART TWO

SACRIFICE

5

Dance with Death

For God so loved the world that he
gave his one and only Son.

John 3:16

In a crowded locker room at Arrowhead Pond in Anaheim, California, forty men in jeans, cowboy hats, and boots prepare to ply their unusual and dangerous trade. Some are stretching tired muscles or rubbing resin on their ropes. Others are adjusting their gloves, spurs, or mouthpieces. Some are simply sitting in front of their lockers with headphones on, lost in either their music or their own thoughts. The air is thick with off-color jokes and macho back talk, but beneath all that is something else—a growing sense of excitement and anxiety.

These men are part of what is known as the "toughest sport on dirt." They are professional bull riders. Each week, these modern-day gladiators enter a packed arena somewhere in the country to test themselves against each other and the fury of a two-thousand-pound bucking beast. Their goal is simple—to stay on an angry, writhing animal for eight full seconds. When they win, the rewards are glory, money, pride, and hero treatment. When they lose, it means no paycheck for another week—or worse.

Injuries are part of any sport, but bull riding is especially brutal on its contestants. During the finals the year before, one rider competed with a partially collapsed lung. Others were riding within weeks of suffering a broken rib, a punctured lung, or a skull fracture. The US professional rodeo circuit averages one to two deaths annually.

It is not an exercise for the timid.

On this day in Anaheim—February 14, 2004—Todd Pierce senses the tension and anticipation in the locker room. He understands it as well as anyone present. For six years, Pierce was a professional bareback horseman competing in rodeos across the country. He was one of the best, consistently ranked among the top twenty in the world.

Today, however, the thirty-three-year-old isn't a competitor. He's a pastor.

Pierce approaches a man applying tape to his gloves and claps him on the back. "Hey, how're you doing?"

"Hey, Todd," the cowboy answers with a smile.

Pierce lowers his voice. "What's been going on? How're the wife and family?"

The question is more than small talk. A career in professional bull riding can easily strain a marriage. It is a lonely as well as dangerous life. The season runs from January through November, so riders are on the road nearly all year. Young fans, many of them female, follow the riders from one venue to another as if they are rock stars. Financial pressures are ever-present for all but the most successful.

In the locker room, the cowboy with Pierce hesitates, then lowers his own voice. "Well, since you asked . . ." He launches into a discussion of a conflict he's been having with his wife.

The conversation is interrupted by a shout from one of the riders: "Let's pray!" Immediately, everyone in the room stops what they're doing. Most either bow their heads or drop to one knee.

There is a thriving Christian faction among the riders. More than a third of the tour members regularly participate in prayer meetings and Bible studies led by Pierce and others. But in the locker room, when the opportunity to meet one's maker may be only minutes away, everyone joins in.

Twenty-four-year-old Wiley Petersen stands to lead the group in prayer. Petersen is in his sixth year on the tour and is one of its rising stars. Last year he finished third in the overall standings, earning nearly $240,000.

"Dear God," Petersen says with eyes closed, "we pray for safety for everyone here today, and that you would be glorified through the things we do. We ask that we ride not only for earthly prizes but for eternal prizes, and that the people in the stands would not be just entertained but inspired."

Thirty minutes later, an announcer in a cowboy hat walks into the center of the arena. "Helloooo, Anaheim!" he yells. Fifteen thousand people yell back. It's time for some bull riding.

Pierce stays close to the action by hanging around the bucking chute where the cowboys mount their bulls. He talks to several of the riders, offering words of encouragement, and sometimes assists in their final preparations.

Pierce knows what's pulsing through their minds and veins—a thrilling mix of adrenaline, excitement, pressure, and fear. He's been drawn to rodeo-style competition since his college days at Idaho State University. Pierce was a pole-vaulter on the track team and in his spare time raced as a horse jockey. About the time he gave up both of those sports, he decided to give rodeo bareback riding a try and loved it.

Also during his years at Idaho State, Pierce experienced an even bigger life change. Though raised in a Christian home, Pierce felt he'd "outgrown" his faith by the time he reached college. During his junior year, when a staff member of Campus Crusade for Christ told him that Jesus Christ loved him and had a plan for his life, Pierce pounded the table and said, "I appreciate what you guys are doing here, but I've got to go."

Yet Pierce couldn't get the Campus Crusade staffer's words out of his head. He realized that he *did* believe in Jesus. It wasn't long before he was committing his life to Christ. Soon after, Leslie, the girlfriend who became his wife, did the same. After graduation, they concluded that God was calling them to a life in professional rodeo. Todd's fellow riders would be their mission field.

On a bucking bronco, Pierce was a natural. He was as gifted as any rider in the country. His first year, he finished third in the standings among rookie riders with the Professional Rodeo Cowboys Association. He was also a three-time Wilderness Circuit champion. Despite his talent, however, the risks of rodeo riding soon caught up with him. It started when a horse fell on him, causing a double fracture in his lower arm and leading to the insertion of a metal plate. Once that healed and Pierce was released to ride, he rebroke the same arm in a different spot. Pierce endured a year and a half of bone grafts and the reinsertion of a plate to heal this time.

Then Pierce broke a finger on his riding hand, which he rebroke two more times. That was followed by a right knee injury, which included torn anterior and posterior cruciate ligaments.

The final blow occurred at the Calgary Stampede in 2000 when Pierce reinjured the same knee. The subsequent surgery triggered the flare-up of a rare nerve disorder that eventually took him to the famous Mayo Clinic in Minnesota. When doctors told Pierce he faced at least a year of recovery time, he knew it was time to hang up his competitive spurs.

Retirement placed Pierce at a crossroads. Rodeo wasn't the most important thing in his life—God, his wife, and his family (two young boys) held that position. But his niche for serving the Lord had been sharing his faith with fellow riders on the rodeo circuit. What was he supposed to do now?

The answer began to materialize when Todd was asked to speak at a rodeo ministry event. One thing led to another;

soon Todd was back on the tour—not as a competitor, but as a pastor for the Professional Bull Riders Association (PBRA). He began to see the purpose for all those injuries.

"Had I done better on a competitive level," Pierce says, "it may have been the very thing that prevented me from doing what God was calling me to do."

Back at the Anaheim Open, Pierce continues to answer the Lord's call. He's been asked to "pull rope" at the bucking chute for B. J. Kramps, a friend and fellow Christian. Kramps, at twenty-six, is a veteran of the sport and former Canadian champion.

In the tight quarters of the chute at the right corner of the arena, there's barely room for a young, tan-colored bull named Double Bogey. From outside the chute, Kramps climbs up and straddles the bull, careful to sit well back of his potentially lethal horns. The bull already has a rope around its middle. Pierce, standing on the arena side of a six-foot metal fence that separates the crowd from the arena, cinches the rope tight and hands the end to Kramps, who slips his gloved left hand under the rope and wraps the end of the rope around his hand.

Kramps nods, the chute opens, and suddenly they're in the arena, spinning and bucking together, bull and cowboy beginning their brief and violent dance with death.

Pierce watches as the bull makes three jumps and then gyrates left in a repeating spin. Kramps stays in control for the full eight seconds, his left hand secure on the rope atop Double Bogey's back, his right arm continuously lifted toward the sky. It's a strong ride, one that will merit a high score.

Pierce turns away to pull the rope for the next rider in the chute. A gasp from the crowd causes him to glance back.

Double Bogey isn't finished yet. By repeating his leftward spin, the side on which Kramps must dismount to easily untangle from the rope, he's put his rider in a pickle. When the bull keeps spinning and Kramps finally dismounts on the right, his left hand is caught in the rope.

Three bullfighters—the bull-riding equivalent of rodeo clowns, the courageous men charged with protecting fallen riders—move in. But the bull, instead of bucking and staying close, takes off running, dragging Kramps beneath him.

At the far end of the arena, the bull turns and charges back to where he started, outrunning the bullfighters. He reaches the corner of the arena at Pierce's left and then rumbles along the fence toward the bucking chute.

Pierce's gut tightens. Kramps, still being dragged, kicked, and stepped on by the bull, appears unconscious. *Oh my gosh*, Pierce thinks. *B. J.'s gettin' killed.*

The beast roars closer. Pierce doesn't stop to consider the risk, the potential to aggravate past injuries, or anything else. When Double Bogey is alongside, Pierce leaps over the bull's back and tries to grab the rope that's ensnared Kramps.

He misses.

He falls into the dirt.

The bull stops at the arena's right corner less than twenty feet away. He turns and sees Pierce.

Pierce scrambles to his feet. The three bullfighters are closing in from the middle of the arena. Kramps is still on the ground, still attached to the bull. Pierce and Double Bogey are eye to eye.

He's got nowhere to go, the pastor thinks, *but through me.*

The bull charges, head low to the ground. Pierce runs forward to meet him. Just before collision, Pierce dives above Double Bogey's head. He's trying to grab the rope and avoid those deadly horns at the same time. With help from the bull, he's flung up and over.

This time, somehow, Pierce succeeds. At the same moment, one of the bullfighters catches up and also grabs hold of the rope. Together, they quickly free Kramps.

Pierce smothers Kramps with his body to protect him from further injury. The bullfighters distract the bull. Soon the animal is corralled. The danger is past.

Pierce looks down at Kramps, fearing the worst. Kramps opens his eyes. In a typical cowboy deadpan, he says, "You can get off me now."

As far as Pierce is concerned, jumping into the arena to save a fellow rider is no big deal. "When you're filled with the love of God, your knee-jerk reaction is to go to someone's aid," he says. "When you're compelled to love, you just do it."

Kramps's extra-long ride results in a mild concussion, but no serious injuries. Later that night, after he's been patched up by a doctor, he and Pierce join other bull riders for a time of Bible study. There's no mention of the incident. It's just another day on the bull riding circuit. Right now it's time to pray. Soon enough, it will be time to prepare for the next dance with death.

Would You? Could You?

(Share your answers if you're reading in a group)

When he saw a fellow cowboy and friend in trouble, Todd Pierce didn't hesitate—he jumped in to do what he could. He put his body and even his life on the line. Though he escaped without injury, he still faced other consequences—a reprimand and a thousand-dollar fine from the PBRA. (Bull riding's powers-that-be frown on the idea of fans or even pastors joining the action in the arena.)

There's a word for what Pierce did. *Wise* isn't it. But *sacrifice* fits the bill.

Sacrifice means many things to people. Some view it as a trade-off—a mom who sacrifices her career to raise her children. Others view it as lost time—a son who sacrifices his Saturday fishing outing with the guys to help his parents clean out the garage. Then there are the rams and lambs presented as burnt offerings in the Old Testament. To people of faith, the purest and most loving form of sacrifice is God the Father allowing his Son to die on the cross for the sins of humanity.

So what does sacrifice mean to you? Let's get into it.

- How about it—if you were literally "on the fence," watching a friend get trampled by an angry bull, *would you* jump down to help? *Could you* do anything to make a difference?

- What's your definition of sacrifice? Is it an obligation? A waste of time? A duty required by God or your parents? An opportunity?
- What's your motivation for sacrifice? Is it a way to impress people or to get something in return? Is it love? What do you think of Todd Pierce's statement about being "compelled to love"?
- The Bible says, "This is love: not that we loved God, but that he loved us and sent his Son as an atoning sacrifice for our sins" (1 John 4:10). What is the connection between sacrifice and love?
- Does the act of sacrifice draw us closer to the Lord? Why or why not?
- Bull riders sacrifice plenty to do what they do, including their health and time with their family. Are they crazy? What do you sacrifice that others might think is crazy? Why do you do it anyway?
- Is there a price for your willingness to sacrifice? If so, what is it?

Reporting In

Sacrifice may be the ultimate act of love. Pray for the Lord's guidance in showing you how to discover that love in your heart and how to show it to others through sacrifice.

Hitting the Trail

(This is just for you)

On his last night with the disciples, Jesus said to them, "My command is this: Love each other as I have loved you. Greater love has no one than this, that he lay down his life for his friends" (John 15:12–13).

According to Christ, the willingness to give up one's life for another is an example of the greatest love of all. But can we "will" such love on our own efforts? Where does this deep love come from?

- Write down the names of people you love enough to give up your life for. Do you think God would have you expand your list?

_____

_____

_____

_____

- The apostle John wrote, "Let us love one another, for love comes from God. Everyone who loves has been born of God and knows God. Whoever does not love does not know God, because God is love" (1 John 4:7–8). Write down what this means to you.

_____

_____

_____

- How can we fully embrace and understand God's love for each of us? Through reading the Bible? Prayer? Meditation? Focusing on others instead of self? List your thoughts, then ask the Lord if he is leading you to any new insights.

_____

_____

_____

71

New Territory

(For those who want to explore further)

Read *Fried Twinkies, Buckle Bunnies, and Bull Riders: A Year Inside the Professional Bull Riders Tour* by Josh Peter. Then attend a professional bull riding event at an arena near you.

- Bull riding has exploded in popularity. Riders compete annually for more than eleven million dollars in prize money, and over one hundred million people watch the sport in person or on TV each year. What is it that's drawing so many fans to bull riding? What's different about bull riding than other sports?
- How do bull riders on the tour sacrifice for each other?

6

A Brotherhood of Faith

A friend loves at all times, and a
brother is born for adversity.

Proverbs 17:17

Hundreds of men are eating or standing in line for
dinner when the captain's voice interrupts, blaring
over loudspeakers throughout the ship: "Now hear
this: Every solider is ordered to sleep with his clothes and life
jacket on. Repeating, this is an order! We have a submarine
following us."

Moments ago, the crew and passengers of the USAT
Dorchester were ribbing each other and enjoying a break
from the ship's routine. Now, after the captain's announce-
ment, every face is grim. They understand they are in deadly
danger.

The date is February 2, 1943. The nations of the world
are in the midst of the second great war of the century. The
nine hundred souls aboard the troop carrier—a mix of army,
navy, coast guard, merchant marine, and civilian person-

nel—launched a few days before from New York, bound for Greenland. They are only about one hundred miles from their destination, but they are in treacherous waters. German U-boats have already sunk scores of Allied ships in the North Atlantic. One was the *Chatham*, a sister ship of the *Dorchester*, the summer before.

The men on the *Dorchester* stare at their food, saying nothing. Then Chaplain George Fox breaks the silence. He stands and announces that it is time for a party. Soon, many of those on board are gathering in the mess hall to try and forget about the stress of the moment. Their attention is focused on four men: Chaplain George Fox, a Methodist who was wounded and decorated in World War I; Chaplain Clark Poling, a Dutch Reformed Protestant and son of a famous radio evangelist; Chaplain Alex Goode, a Jewish rabbi and new father; and the bespectacled Chaplain John Washington, a Catholic priest who had barely survived a mysterious illness while in high school. Washington sits at a dusty piano and the quartet, all blessed with strong voices, leads the group in singing popular tunes.

By now, it is no surprise for the soldiers to see these four men of faith working together so easily. They'd met at the chaplain school at Harvard University and become uncommon friends.

"There was a camaraderie among them that was hard to describe because it was so unexpected," one shipmate later said. "I was raised Catholic in an Irish neighborhood, and there the Catholics didn't talk to any Protestants, and none of us Protestants and Catholics spoke to the few Jews who were there. . . . To see these men in the same uniform but of different faiths getting together and actually talking and laughing and smiling and joking with each other was unheard of."

The personal chemistry among the chaplains is an extension of what they all seem to believe, that the typical separation of religions and clergymen is not what God intended for his people. Rabbi Goode has written and preached for years about his hopes for an interfaith brotherhood that will bind nations and races together despite their differences.

Now, in the mess hall, the chaplains have another opportunity to demonstrate their faith and philosophy. The party continues for hours, finally breaking up about 11:30. The atmosphere is not exactly festive; no one can entirely put aside the gravity of the situation. But at least some of the men leave the room encouraged, humming happy tunes as they return to duty or to their crowded quarters.

As shipboard clocks tick past midnight, Army First Sergeant Michael Warish begins to relax. In a few hours, the *Dorchester* will have air protection from the Allied base at Greenland. They should be landing about 10 a.m. They are so close. They are going to make it.

Warish is making rounds in the soldiers' quarters. He sits on someone's bed—bunks throughout the ship are stacked between three and five beds high—and checks his new wristwatch, a gift from his mother. It reads 12:45 a.m. It's actually ten minutes slow.

"Hey, Sarge," a soldier says to Warish, "what if—"

The soldier is interrupted by a loud crash. A second later, there is a muffled explosion.

The lights go out. Steam hisses out of broken pipes. Men begin screaming. The ship lists to starboard.

Bunk beds, including the one Warish is sitting on, collapse. A heavy beam of wood strikes Warish on the head and back. The bed that was above him now pins his right leg. He tries to lift the bunk, but he can't; he's stuck. In the rest of the quarters, the men who are still alive and mobile scramble for life jackets in the darkness. Some shout, "Where's my clothes?" Then they start stumbling out through the partially jammed door. Warish is being abandoned.

Once again, the U-boats have found a target.

The chaplains are in their bunks when the torpedo hits. At the sound of the explosion, they leap into action. This is their battlefield. In some ways, they are better prepared for the crisis than most on the *Dorchester*. During World War I, Fox had rescued fallen comrades from a gas-infested area. As a child, Goode saved his siblings from a house fire. Washington's earlier brush with death made him faithful and fearless. Poling felt he had met God on a mountaintop and was more ready than ever to serve him. The chaplains are soon on deck, handing out life jackets to panicked soldiers.

Navy gunner Roy Summers, a survivor of the *Chatham* sinking, secures a life jacket of his own on the top deck, where he finds the last one in a storage site. He puts it on and runs aft, intending to jump off. The screams from that end of the ship change his mind, however. In the darkness, some of the men have unwittingly jumped into the still-turning propeller.

Summers runs in the other direction, where he encounters two of the chaplains talking with two soldiers at a railing. They're trying to get the soldiers to lower themselves by rope to a lifeboat in the water below, but one of the young soldiers is hysterical. One of the chaplains—Summers can't identify who it is in the blackness—shakes the hysterical boy, then slaps him.

"I want you to take this jacket, get on the lifeline, and drop off the ship," the chaplain says. "You can save yourself."

The panicked soldier grabs the chaplain by the neck as if to strangle him. Summers intervenes and pulls the soldier away. "Come with me," Summers says. "We can go down the rope together." But the soldier breaks away and runs down the sloping deck toward the propeller.

Before he climbs down the rope himself, Summers observes the chaplains encouraging others to overcome their fear and abandon ship.

Chaplain Washington, after offering absolution to the departing men, urges Private First Class Charles Macli to get into the water as well. "Father, get off the ship yourself!" Macli yells. "It's going down!"

"No," Washington says. "But *you* must get off."

Macli does not stay to argue. He slides into the frigid ocean.

A few moments later, soldier Water Miller walks up and down the deck, looking for an opening at the railing. He knows he must get off the sinking ship, but the railing is blocked by a crowd of men two and three deep, all too terrified to move. Some are groaning or weeping.

A loud and panicked voice penetrates the haunting sounds: "I can't find my life jacket. I can't find my life jacket."

Miller turns to look and hears another voice: "Here's one, soldier." The man behind the second voice unhooks his life jacket and helps the frightened soldier put it on. It's too dark for Miller to make out faces, but he recognizes the voice of Chaplain Fox.

Hugh Moffett, a member of the merchant marine, witnesses a similar scene. Moffett is lowering a lifeboat filled with men when he sees Chaplain Washington grab a nearby soldier without a life jacket. Washington slips off his life jacket and helps the soldier into it.

"God bless you, Father," the soldier says. He moves to the railing.

At about this time, Navy Lieutenant John Mahoney is on deck, swearing at himself for leaving his gloves in his cabin. He turns to go after them, but a voice calls him back.

"Don't bother, Mahoney. I have another pair. You can have these." Chaplain Goode pulls off his gloves and hands them to Mahoney. The lieutenant tries to say no, but Goode insists that he has a second pair. Mahoney puts on the gloves and lowers himself into the water.

Mahoney ends up in a lifeboat for the next eight hours. It is frequently filled with freezing water, chilling its occupants to death. The lieutenant later says he never would have made it without the gloves. Of the forty men in the lifeboat, he is one of only two survivors.

On another part of the deck, Second Engineer Grady Clark observes another chaplain in action. He is forcing his life jacket over the head of a protesting soldier, who knows what the sacrifice will mean for the chaplain. "I don't want your jacket!" the soldier yells.

The chaplains all carry the rank of lieutenant. This one now uses his authority: "Get into it, soldier, and get into it fast!"

With the soldier in the life jacket, the chaplain pushes him with an open hand down the tilting deck and against the rail. The chaplain then lifts the soldier over the rail and into the ocean. He turns and spies Clark.

"Soldier, what are you doing here?" the chaplain says. "Get over the rail." The chaplain spins Clark around and stays with him until Clark climbs over.

"Swim out!" he calls to Clark, and laughs strangely.

Grady Clark isn't sure which chaplain has urged him out to sea. He does not know that Clark Poling is known for having a funny, nervous laugh when afraid or angry.

Merchant marine Daniel O'Keefe is paddling in the icy water when someone pulls him into an already crowded lifeboat. A minute later, he sees a man without a life jacket standing on the listing deck of the *Dorchester*. "So long, boys," the man calls. "Good luck!"

O'Keefe recognizes the voice of Chaplain Fox.

Meanwhile, Michael Warish is still fighting for his life. For ten minutes after the torpedo hit, he tried to move the collapsed bunk that had pinned his foot. Suddenly his foot worked free. He tested it and realized it was broken. In pain, Warish had crawled to the door and eventually to the deck. The sea on the port side of the ship was filled with blinking red lights; each life jacket was equipped with a battery-powered light to aid night rescuers. Warish realized there was no need for rescue, however. Everyone he could see was dead.

Now, limping to the starboard side of the ship, Warish comes across a group tending to a wounded man. The four chaplains are among them. Rabbi Goode, the only chaplain

still with a life jacket, takes his off and kneels down beside
the injured man, who is lying on the deck. The rabbi unlaces
his boots, slips the man's one good shoulder through the life
jacket, then uses his laces to tie the other side of the jacket
around the man's injured shoulder.

Goode then joins the other three chaplains, who are standing against a bulkhead. They begin to pray in a strange mix-
ture of English, Hebrew, and Latin. The icy Atlantic splashes
ever higher on the listing and sinking deck. With the chaplains' prayer ringing in his ears, Warish jumps into the water
and is pulled to safety by someone on a life raft.

Just twenty minutes after the U-boat's torpedo struck the
Dorchester, the troop ship makes its fatal plunge into the
ocean. Private First Class James Eardley, from his vantage
point on a life raft, is watching. The ship rolls over, and
suddenly he spies the four chaplains. They have climbed
onto the keel and are standing there arm in arm. Then the
Dorchester noses down and the chaplains disappear from
view.

Of the nine hundred men on board the *Dorchester* that
night, only two hundred thirty will survive the U-boat attack. Yet the four chaplains, through their calm, their encouragement, and their determination to give up their lives
for others, are credited with saving many of those who do
survive.

Grady Clark, who was urged out to sea by one of the
chaplains, later wrote in an affidavit to the US Army, "As I
left the ship, I looked back and saw the chaplains . . . with
their hands clasped, praying for the boys. They never made
any attempt to save themselves, but they did try to save the
others. I think their names should be on the list of 'The
Greatest Heroes of this war.'"

Another survivor, Private First Class John Ladd, was
equally moved by the actions of the chaplains that terrible
night in the Atlantic. He described them as "the finest thing
I have seen or hope to see this side of heaven."

Would You? Could You?

(Share your answers if you're reading in a group)

If the crucible of crisis shows what we are truly made of, then hundreds of men in the North Atlantic were given the opportunity for self-discovery on February 3, 1943. The reactions certainly varied. A kitchen worker, wildly waving a meat cleaver to clear his path to a boat, was shot to death by an officer before he could slice up his comrades. Other men fought each other for positions in lifeboats and rafts. Roy Summers, who saved the unidentified chaplain from a hysterical soldier, jumped into the water and was beaten by a man wielding an oar when he tried to climb aboard a lifeboat. Many other men, meanwhile, were simply frozen in fear. They remained on deck till the end, too petrified to even attempt saving themselves.

The chaplains were not alone in their heroism. Some men in rafts continued to pull survivors out of the sea, even when fellow passengers protested that they would capsize the craft. Others on the convoy's rescuing ships bravely risked their lives to help the chilled survivors from the ocean. Yet the performance of the chaplains stood out. From the moment the torpedo hit, they seemed almost eager to give up their chance for survival. The chaplains had plenty to live for. Three were married and had children at home. The fourth, Washington, was the eldest sibling of a large family. They had friends and congregations who looked up to them, as well as dreams for serving the Lord in the future. Yet when the *Dorchester* was attacked, none of that seemed to matter.

The case can be made that once we invite the Lord into our hearts, we have already surrendered our lives to him, and the rest of our time on earth is simply an extension of our commitment and faith. The chaplains had already given their lives to God. For them, sacrifice was almost second nature. How about you?

- If you were on board the *Dorchester* after the U-boat attack, *would you* be more concerned about the fate of your shipmates or your own survival? *Could you* give up your life jacket to a fellow soldier, even someone you don't know?

- One survivor later said of the chaplains, "How they were able to let their love for God overwhelm their love for their lives was an act of faith." Do you agree or disagree with that statement? Why?

- Jesus Christ said to his disciples, "If anyone would come after me, he must deny himself and take up his cross and follow me. For whoever wants to save his life will lose it, but whoever loses his life for me will find it" (Matt. 16:24–25). What does Jesus mean by this? What did the chaplains "find" by their final actions on the *Dorchester*?

- In 1943, most Americans focused more on their differences in beliefs than on their commonalities. How does war break down such differences? How can unity move us toward a life of sacrifice? Is it possible to go too far in unity?

- Do you think the chaplains were scared that night? Do you think their faith wavered? How might they have encouraged each other during the crisis? Apart from the four men who received life jackets from the chaplains (and who apparently did not survive), how did the actions and sacrifices of the chaplains encourage others around them? How does having a brother standing by you provide strength for a crisis?

- When has someone else's sacrifice inspired you? When has your own sacrifice made a difference in someone else's life?

Reporting In

Is the Lord asking you to make any sacrifices in your life today? Why don't you sit down and ask him.

Hitting the Trail

(This is just for you)

You may believe in the importance of sacrifice. You may be able to point to some great examples of how you've served others at your own expense. Some of us, however, are selective about our sacrifice. We choose only the "deserving" beneficiaries. What is so inspiring about the four chaplains on the *Dorchester* is that they did not stop to help only those they knew or who seemed to need aid the most. They gave up their life jackets for random soldiers and tried to help and encourage *everyone*. Is that your kind of sacrifice?

- Think about your recent acts of service and sacrifice. Who are the people or type of people you usually help? Who do you usually avoid? Why is that?

  _____

  _____

  _____

- Sacrifice, by definition, isn't convenient or easy. Maybe it's time for you to be bolder in the area of sacrifice. Make a list of bold steps you could take that would change the lives of others. Now write down how you think these steps might change your faith and life.

  _____

  _____

  _____

- Have you thought lately about what Jesus's sacrifice on the cross is really about? Do you see a similarity between what he did and what the chaplains did? Are you moved by the image of Christ on the cross or does it feel like ancient history? If the latter, what can you do to change that?

_____

_____

_____

New Territory

(For those who want to explore further)

Read Dan Kurzman's *No Greater Glory*, an account of the four chaplains and the 1943 *Dorchester* disaster. Watch the DVD documentary *The Four Chaplains: Sacrifice at Sea* produced by Faith & Values Media.

- Which of the four chaplains do you most admire or relate to? Why?
- In terms of unity, brotherhood, and faith, how is our world different than it was in 1943? How is it still the same?

7

Blowup

To gain that which is worth having, it may
be necessary to lose everything else.

Bernadette Devlin

Don Mackey and his team of seven smoke jumpers are finding unexpected trouble. They've just parachuted into a canyon that's steeper and more slippery than it appeared from the air. It's getting dark. Logs outlined by winking embers are crashing down around them as they begin cutting a fire line. Then a boulder tumbles past. Mackey gives the order to turn around, saying, "There's nothing on this hill worth getting killed over."

The smoke jumpers are on Storm King Mountain in Colorado. Mackey is smoke jumper-in-charge of the team from Missoula, Montana. At thirty-four, he has a younger man's face and an athlete's build. More important to the rest of the crew, he's a storyteller, is always ready with an encouraging word, and has eight years of experience as a smoke jumper.

The others are glad he's with them on this fire. Some have an uneasy feeling. Smoke jumpers are the special forces of firefighters, commandos who swoop in, attack, and move on. But on this night—July 5, 1994—the fire has spread to fifty acres, more than their lone team can handle. At 11 p.m., Mackey radios a request for an additional forty firefighters by morning. On a stretch of real estate named Hell's Gate Ridge, as the rest of the smoke jumpers try to find a comfortable place to sleep, Mackey stays up late into the night, watching the fire.

In the morning, another team of smoke jumpers parachutes in. Mackey joins incident commander Butch Blanco of the Bureau of Land Management (BLM) in a helicopter for a view of the fire. What they see isn't good. The fire has doubled in size to one hundred acres.

Blanco and Mackey talk it over and decide Mackey should start a fire line at the top of the ridge, move downhill along the ridge's west flank, and encircle the fire. The beginning of the maneuver will include some risk; before them is a thick patch of scrub Gambel oak, pinyon pine, and juniper. But Mackey tells a fellow jumper that once they get past the heavy vegetation and start moving down and parallel to the ridge, they'll find more sparse terrain.

Soon Mackey's smoke jumpers are hard at work. They are joined by nine members of the Prineville (Oregon) Hot Shots, part of an elite team assigned to battle the largest fires, as well as another group of firefighters. What they don't know is that an updated weather forecast, a "red flag warning" issued at 12:30 that afternoon, calls for a front to move in, accompanied by gusts and a sudden shift in wind direction. The warning reaches the BLM office in Grand Junction, but the staff there is overworked and dealing with numerous fires. The message is lost. The firefighters on Storm King Mountain never hear it.

Cutting the fire line is slow going. At one point, the flexible oak kicks the chain off smoke jumper Tony Petrilli's chain saw. Mackey, one of his best friends, approaches. Mackey enjoys reminding Petrilli that it was his job to grade Petrilli's sawyer-qualification test. Now Mackey offers to help, but a cold stare from Petrilli stops him. Petrilli repairs the chain and slices off a twig.

"Did I do that just right, Don?" he says.

Mackey laughs and moves on.

At 2 p.m., there are twenty-four firefighters on the west flank of Hell's Gate Ridge. They stop for a break, and Mackey turns to Keith Erickson, another experienced smoke jumper who also happens to be Mackey's brother-in-law. In a kidding tone, Mackey asks who Erickson thinks is in charge of the fire, himself or Blanco.

"I don't know," Erickson says.

"Me neither. Do you want the fire?"

"I'll take it if you want to give it to me."

Mackey doesn't answer for a moment. "Nah," he says. "We'll see what happens later."

Erickson isn't sure if his brother-in-law is still kidding or not. It's a sign that the usually confident Mackey is growing increasingly uncomfortable with the expansion of the fire and his responsibilities.

Sometime later, Mackey flips on his radio. "The wind's getting a little girly down here," he says.

Smoke jumper Sarah Doehring, another friend of Mackey's, overhears the report and can't help teasing him about it. "*Girly*, Don?" she says with a laugh.

Mackey corrects his error. "The wind's getting *squirrely*," he says.

The wind, in fact, is shifting and gathering strength. The front is arriving.

It makes its introduction far out of sight of the firefighters, to the south, on the floor of the drainage on the west side of Hell's Gate Ridge. It's a place where, in one of the driest summers in years, some sections of pine trees and scrub oak are already alight from windblown embers and creeping fire from higher on the ridge. They're burning slowly, but that's about to change.

When conditions are just right, what firefighters call a blowup can ignite in seconds and destroy everything in its path. Steep terrain on both sides of a gulch or canyon acts as a chimney, funneling the flame in a single direction and generating heat nearing two thousand degrees Fahrenheit. In 1871, during another exceptionally dry season, forest fires combined with tornado-force winds to incinerate the town of Peshtigo, Wisconsin, killing more than twelve hundred people. In 1949, in a remote Montana canyon named Mann Gulch, thirteen smoke jumpers lost their lives trying to outrun a blowup. Every firefighter on Storm King Mountain knows the history of Mann Gulch—and that no smoke jumper has been claimed by fire since.

At 4 p.m., Mackey and twelve other firefighters—three smoke jumpers and nine Prineville Hot Shots—are spread out along the western flank of the fire line, farthest from the ridge. Another group of nine smoke jumpers, including Petrilli, is south of them and closer to the ridge. Erickson and four other firefighters are positioned north and near the top of the canyon, two hundred feet from the ridge, while Blanco and eighteen more firefighters are at the top of Hell's Gate Ridge. Further north on the ridge are two helicopter crewmen and the Prineville Hot Shot superintendent. A total of forty-nine people are scattered along the southern reaches of Storm King Mountain.

The firefighters are tired and hungry. Some are concerned about the increased fire activity and unusual winds. But no one realizes what's about to happen.

A little after 4 p.m., a mighty west wind blows into the gorge cut by the Colorado River and is funneled into the western drainage. Compressed into the chimney of the drainage, the wind increases in strength and hits the small fires there.

The wind, the shape of the drainage, and the dry vegetation combine to make something perfect and terrible. The flames explode. The sound is like a jet plane. The fire's sudden fury has nowhere to go but north, up the drainage.

It's a blowup.

On his spot below the ridge, Petrilli sees it. He grabs his radio and punches Mackey's frequency.

"The fire's spotted across the canyon, and it's roaring."

"Is it across the *main* canyon?" Mackey asks.

"Yes, it's across the main canyon. It's rolling, and we're getting out of here."

Petrilli looks at the drainage one more time. In the short time he's been on the radio, the flame front has advanced fifty yards. He marches toward higher ground, a place they've named Lunch Spot Ridge, still below the main ridge. As he crests the ridge, he sees Mackey arriving from the other side. His friend's eyes are red and tearing from smoke.

Mackey waves. "Go up, there's good black farther up!"

Petrilli moves to Mackey's side.

"Where's Longanecker?" Mackey is asking about the line scout who was with Petrilli's group. He presses his radio to his mouth: "Dale, are you okay?"

"Yes" is the terse reply.

Mackey and Longanecker discuss the other west flank firefighters. They're at serious risk. Mackey says he's going back to "check on them" or "to get those people out." Later, Longanecker can't remember the exact wording.

Petrilli moves up the ridge for fifty yards. He turns around, assuming Mackey is behind him. Smoke is obscuring the view of the west flank line below him. Mackey isn't there.

Petrilli waits a moment, then thinks, *I'd better go.* He turns and continues up the ridge.

Mackey, back at the west end of Lunch Spot Ridge, finishes his radio call with Longanecker. He's thinking about the firefighters on the west flank. He raises his radio again: "Okay, everybody out of the canyon."

Mackey could easily follow Petrilli and the others up Lunch Spot Ridge. Instead, he moves down into the drainage. Through smoke and increasing heat, he reaches the spot where he left the smoke jumpers, but they've either seen the fire or heard his warning and are already moving north up the drainage. They're gone.

Mackey is known for his ability to power hike. He uses it now and in a few minutes catches up with the single-file line. He knows the fire is behind him; he can hear it and feel it. But the smoke, the choppy terrain in the drainage, and the thick scrub oak make it difficult to see exactly how close the fire is. Ahead of Mackey, three smoke jumpers and the nine Prineville Hot Shots are marching briskly uphill toward the top of the drainage, Hell's Gate Ridge. They're concerned, increasing their pace with each glance back, but not panicked. Everyone still carries tools or chain saws.

In the first minutes, the smoke jumpers gain on the fire. But the blowup races through a half-acre of heavy brush and accelerates. At about this time, the firefighters reach a spur ridge about two hundred yards from the top of Hell's Gate Ridge. It slows them down.

One of the firefighters is six-foot-four-inch Eric Hipke, a hockey player from Washington State. He's third in line. When their path splits and goes around a tree, he considers passing the two men in front. He holds back. It doesn't feel right.

Near the top of the spur ridge, Hipke turns for a glance back. He's surprised to see Mackey at the rear of the line. Mackey is straining from the exertion; he's just hiked and jogged a quarter mile up the drainage. His eyes meet Hipke's and deliver an urgent message: *Go! Go!*

Erickson, Mackey's brother-in-law, is standing near the top of the drainage with smoke jumper Brad Haugh. Two hundred feet of steep slope separates them from Hell's Gate Ridge. "Shouldn't we be getting out of here?" Erickson asks.

"Let's hold on," Haugh says. He expects the west flank firefighters to arrive soon. "Let's give them a little support, maybe grab a saw or lend a hand."

The firefighters come into view below, about 150 yards away. Mackey's black hat is visible, now second from the end of the line. "Come on, guys, get moving. You've got fire down there!" Erickson shouts into his radio.

Inexplicably, when the retreating firefighters are about one hundred yards from where Erickson and Haugh watch from above, they pause a few moments before resuming their uphill journey. Suddenly, Erickson sees fire emerge downslope, a threat to cut off Mackey and his group.

"There's a spot below you guys," he radios. "Get up here now!"

Haugh is waving his arms and yelling at the firefighters. "Drop your tools! Run!"

Erickson feels a hand on his shoulder. "Let's get out of here!" Haugh shouts. Haugh races up and over the ridge, thinking, *So this is what it's like to run for your life.* Erickson follows, being chased by a flame front 150 feet high. He is a few yards from the top when a blast of heat slams into his back. He screams and scrambles over.

Moments before, Hipke was still third in the line of firefighters when the man in the lead reached a slightly wider point on the drainage trail. The firefighter stopped, stepped to the side, and said, "Shelter?"

Hipke saw his chance. With an inferno on its way, he wasn't going to risk deploying the aluminum-foil shelter that every firefighter carries. He burst through the opening like an attacking wingman and ran as fast as his legs would carry him toward the ridge. He was focused on one goal: *Get out! Get out! Get out!*

A roar engulfs Hipke. He can feel his skin burning. He covers his ears with his hands. He scrambles up the slope. He's twenty, fifteen, ten yards from the ridge.

The heat intensifies to a searing level. He moves his hands to cover his face.

This is it.

Hipke dives forward and screams. Before he hits the ground, he's struck by a wave of superheated energy that knocks off his hard hat and burns the back side of his body.

But it lasts only a moment. He hasn't caught the full intensity of the blowup. The skin on his hands hangs in loose threads, but he can stand. He stumbles over the ridge and finds Erickson and Haugh.

"Where is everybody else?" he asks.

Everybody else—the firefighters racing for their lives toward Hell's Gate Ridge—didn't make it. Nine Prineville Hot Shots and three Missoula smoke jumpers are dead. Two more helicopter crewmen perish near the peak of Storm King Mountain. Later, the body of one of the Hot Shots is found just one hundred feet from the ridge. Don Mackey, smoke-jumper-in-charge and friend of just about everyone who knows him, is found in a surprisingly different place.

Mackey was somehow partially protected from the initial wave of flame, perhaps by the bodies of other firefighters. He left his pack and walked downhill through the blowup, the closest thing to hell on earth. It's possible that he couldn't see and had no idea where he was going. It's also possible that he knew he was dead, and he decided to round up his crew one final time. He passed the charred bodies of two firefighters and kept walking until he reached the last of his team, Hot Shot Bonnie Holtby, already gone. There, at 4:13 p.m., Don Mackey knelt to the ground, put his head on his folded arms, and died.

Would You? Could You?

(Share your answers if you're reading in a group)

Nothing is quite like the life of a smoke jumper. Scott Belknap, then a thirteen-year veteran, once said of his occupation, "There is nothing as exciting, nothing in the world like jumping into an area where no other human being has been . . . Everyone here is an adventurer. And I think everybody here has that Peter Pan Syndrome: they don't want to grow up. We're physical people who don't like the idea of slowing down. So this is really the greatest job in the world."

Taking part in the world's greatest job also carries a great deal of responsibility, however, especially if you're a squad boss, a smoke-jumper-in-charge, or an incident commander. Conditions can change in a hurry, and when mistakes are made, lives may be lost. Those in authority are responsible for the safety of their crews. Don Mackey must have felt the weight of that charge in 1994 on Storm King Mountain. But how far does that responsibility go? And is it worth dying for?

- What if you were Don Mackey? With a fire on its way, *would you* return to the west flank to make sure your crew was on its way out? *Could you* do it knowing a blowup was imminent? *Could you* forgive yourself if you survived and the rest of your team did not?
- Mackey had just been promoted to a career position as a firefighter, and Storm King was his first jump of the season. He might have wanted to impress his superiors and let them know they'd made a wise decision. Could that have altered his judgment on Storm King? Would it alter yours? When is ambition healthy and when is it not?
- Experience and maturity often—though not always—counteract the influence of excitement and adrenaline during a crisis. Which had the most influence on Storm King Mountain? Did the firefighters ignore obvious warning signs? Would you have responded differently?
- Read the parable of the Good Samaritan in Luke 10:25–37. How were Mackey's actions on Storm King like the Good Samaritan's? How were they different?
- Brad Haugh originally planned to offer a helping hand to the escaping firefighters, but when he saw the flame front closing in, he abandoned the idea and ran for the ridge. Did he make the right choice? Why or why not?
- Jesus said that the second of the two greatest commandments is "Love your neighbor as yourself" (Matt. 22:39).

93

How great is your love for your "neighbor"? *Would you* honestly risk your life for him or her? What if it's 90 percent likely that you'll die in the attempt? Seventy-five percent likely? Fifty-fifty? Should your answer depend on whether you are single versus married with children at home?

- When has someone taken a personal risk—physical or otherwise—to help you during a crisis? How did you feel about that person's actions? Have you ever been ready to or actually have put your life at risk for someone else? How did that make you feel about yourself?

Reporting In

Are you struggling with any of these issues? It's time to pray for guidance. Has God given you clear direction? It's still time to pray!

Hitting the Trail

(This is just for you)

Most of us won't be parachuting into a fire anytime soon, so we probably won't have to deal with firefighters trying to escape a blowup. Yet we know any number of people who are in distress. In some cases it's obvious; in others, they try to hide it. Either way, for them the crisis is real. So . . . what are you going to do about it?

- Make a list of people you know who might be in distress. What is their issue? What do they need? What is your plan to do something about it? Write it down here.

_____

_____

_____

- What situations are most likely to draw you in as a Good Samaritan? When are you least likely to step in? How is your reluctance in that area affecting your relationships with family and friends? What could you do to change that? Record it here.

  _____

  _____

  _____

- In what ways, if any, would you like to be more like Don Mackey? Write them down, and then write how you could make that happen.

  _____

  _____

  _____

New Territory

(For those who want to explore further)

Read *Fire on the Mountain*, John Maclean's account of the fire on Storm King Mountain, and Norman Maclean's *Young Men and Fire*, the story of the 1949 Mann Gulch fire.

- How were these two tragedies comparable? How were they different?
- Do you have what it takes to be a smoke jumper? Why or why not?

8

With Gladness

Serve the LORD with gladness;
Come before His presence with singing.

Psalm 100:2 NKJV

Only three exhausted, starving hostages are left, hiking through the soggy jungle with their captors. Over the past year, the rest of the twenty-four Filipino and American hostages have either been released for ransom payments, abandoned after being wounded in one of the frequent gun battles with government troops, or beheaded.

It's June 7, 2002, on Mindanao in the Philippines, a large island of volcanic mountains and swampy lowland plateaus that is home to most of the country's Muslims. One year and eleven days ago, armed members of a militant Islamic separatist group called Abu Sayyaf kidnapped tourists from their beds at a nearby beach resort to extort money for their radical cause.

Martin and Gracia Burnham had been celebrating their eighteenth wedding anniversary at that resort, a rare vacation indulgence given their modest income running an aviation service for the New Tribes Mission in Mindanao. Since the mid-1980s, Martin has flown in food and medicine to the natives and missionaries and has transported tribal patients to medical facilities.

When he was flying his missions, there had always been risk, and Gracia had been his ground crew, staying in constant communication by radio. But today, on this rainy afternoon in the jungle, they are side by side, physically spent by the most dangerous ordeal of their lives. Martin is a bearded skeleton compared to the handsome, fun-loving pilot who swept Gracia off her feet two decades ago.

"I just don't think I can keep doing this much longer," Gracia tells him.

"You know, Gracia, I just think we're going to get out of here soon," Martin says. "I think this is all going to work out. After we're home, this is going to seem like such a short time to us. Let's just hold steady."

The words are typical of Martin. He is always ready with more encouragement, always quick to shore up Gracia's flagging spirit.

When Sabaya, an Abu Sayyaf leader who speaks English, gives the order to make camp on the steep downslope of a mountain, Martin and Gracia huddle together in a hammock in the jungle under a makeshift cloth shelter. They do their best to comfort one another, but both know in their hearts that they may die here—that "going home" may mean going to be with their Lord.

On the run from the AFP (Armed Forces of the Philippines), hostages and captors alike are weak today, and they've been lax about covering their tracks. They had to abandon their single cooking pot during a gun battle and have eaten nothing but raw rice and some leaves from the low vegetation for the past nine days. When Sabaya caught some of his men greedily eating more than their fair share of the limited supply, he took all the rice and gave it to Martin to carry. The extra weight made the pack cut deeper into his shoulders.

"He's the only one I can trust who won't eat it," Sabaya had said to Gracia.

Martin didn't complain. He was often made to carry extra supplies, which sometimes made him slip and fall in the mud, but he never complained. When the Abu Sayyaf's satellite phone broke, he repaired it for them. As he served them, he talked to his captors and fellow hostages about his faith in Jesus, and they listened.

Today, as always when they stop to rest, Martin has made sure the other remaining hostage, a Filipino nurse who also had been abducted from the resort, has her hammock secured between sturdy trees. The nurse is settled just a short distance up the hill from Martin and Gracia as they quietly recite memorized Scriptures to one another and sing favorite hymns together in their hammock.

"I really don't know why this has happened to us," Martin says. "I've been thinking a lot lately about Psalm 100—what it says about serving the Lord with gladness. This may not seem much like serving the Lord, but that's what we're doing, you know? We may not leave this jungle alive, but we can leave this world serving the Lord with gladness. We can come before his presence with singing."

Martin and Gracia pray together for their three children back home, thank the Lord for being with them in the midst of all this, and try to take a nap.

Suddenly a stream of gunfire erupts from the top of the hill, very close to their location.

"Oh, God!" Gracia says. She's not swearing. She's praying.

She knows she needs to drop to the ground. As she swings her feet over the side of the hammock, she's aware of a bullet zinging through her right leg. She rolls eight feet down the slope and sees Martin on the ground, twisted into an unnatural position, eyes closed.

It's 1981, back at Calvary Bible College in Kansas City, where Martin and Gracia have known each other as friends for a few years. But Martin catches her off guard when he asks her for a date to the fall concert.

"Can I let you know?" she stammers.

No, you can't. Never mind then. That, he says later, was his rehearsed answer to this dreaded female evasive maneuver.

But what comes out of his mouth is, "Yeah. You can let me know."

He surprises himself with his own response, figures this gal must be something pretty special, then turns and heads for class.

She immediately checks with her girlfriends, who are enthusiastic because everybody agrees Martin is a terrific guy. She accepts.

He shows up wearing a suit she's never seen him in before, but the same cowboy boots he always wears with his flannel shirt and jeans. His dashing moustache matches his reddish hair, and his eyes twinkle at his good fortune to be with this pretty girl tonight. After the concert he takes her flying to see the lights of Kansas City at night.

Definitely his own person, she thinks. *Confident and competent but not the least bit egotistical, and kind to everyone.*

It's the summer of 1983 in the farm town of Imperial, Nebraska, where Martin and Gracia have been head-over-heels-in-love newlyweds for less than a year. They have a great church community, Martin is working as a crop duster, and Gracia is involved in a women's Bible study and taking a class on furniture refinishing.

Martin is offered a permanent job by one of the local farmers.

One beautiful summer evening, he says to Gracia, "You know, it would be so easy to settle down in this community and make a good living, wouldn't it? . . . But that's not what we're called to do."

It's 1985 at the New Tribes Mission flight training base in Arizona, and Martin and Gracia are in a planning meeting with the mission board. "Please send us anywhere except the Philippines," Martin says. "Maybe someplace like Paraguay."

He liked the Philippines just fine, but because that's where he grew up, the old-timers in the New Tribes Mission there would remember him as just the little kid of a missionary. *Would they value his skills and respect him as a pilot? Would they feel safe trusting him with their lives when they flew with him?*

"You know, Martin," a board member says, "they really do need a replacement pilot in the Philippines. You know the culture and you partly know the language. We'd rather not send you someplace else. Would you be willing to go back?"

Gracia watches proudly as her husband nods yes. *He's just that kind of person—willing to serve wherever the call takes him.*

Anyplace will be fine with her, as long as she can be with him.

In the jungle on Mindanao, Gracia is still on the ground in the midst of the gun battle. As she crawls to Martin's side, she sees it.

Oh no! He's been hit.

From Martin's upper left chest, a growing pool of blood is soaking through his white shirt. His breathing is heavy. But he is so still that she takes her cue from him and decides not to yell for help as she normally would have.

The Filipino nurse sees him too. "Mart!" she yells. Then she is silent. She too has been struck by gunfire. She won't speak again.

Gracia lies quietly next to Martin, realizing their best chance to survive is to play dead so the Abu Sayyaf will flee and leave them there. The sounds of whizzing bullets and exploding grenades continue all around them.

Lord, Gracia prays, *if this is it, just make it happen quickly.*

Minutes pass as the shooting rages on. Martin moans softly a few times. Then his body slumps against hers.

The shooting subsides, then stops. She hears shouts in Tagalog, the language of the AFP, but no answering shouts from the members of Abu Sayyaf. *They must have retreated down the mountain.*

All but one of the Abu Sayyaf have escaped. From the start, the AFP had proudly denied the urgent request of the American military to take charge of a night rescue using special forces with night goggles. The Philippine government forbade the United States to intervene on its soil. Instead, the AFP went in with guns blazing in broad daylight and managed to hit all three hostages.

Gracia slowly waves her hand so the soldiers will see her without being startled—so they will not shoot anymore.

Two AFP soldiers struggle on the slippery ground to carry Gracia past the now-tattered shelter and up toward the top of the mountain, where a Black Hawk helicopter is being directed to land. She longs to make time stand still, but she can't. Looking desperately back toward Martin, she sees that the red stain now covers his chest and all color has drained from his face. There is no more breath in her husband's emaciated body.

He has gone on ahead. And she is left to hang on to the words he used to encourage her countless times: "You can do this, Gracia. You've got to go home whole."

She remembers that Martin's backpack has all the notes they wrote during their captivity and his letters to their children—memories of him that they must have.

"Go get that green bag," Gracia says. "I've got to have that. . . . You have to get it!"

The soldiers hesitate, but finally one goes back to retrieve it.

As a medic starts preparing her for the helicopter lift to the hospital, Gracia is suddenly so exhausted she just wants to drift off to sleep.

It's June 13, 2002, in Wichita, Kansas, six days after Martin's death. Gracia has endured a sea of concerned, caring faces at the airport, the hospital, and the American embassy in the Philippines.

She has wrestled with and defeated her bitterness against the AFP for the rescue gone wrong. By the time she met with President Arroyo of the Philippines, the venomous reproach she had contemplated had given way to a spirit of forgiveness that she knew Martin would have wanted.

Getting around in a wheelchair, Gracia has been joyously reunited with their children, and Martin's body has been returned for his funeral tomorrow.

The casket will be closed for the funeral, but it is open tonight for the family viewing. Gracia has done her best to prepare Jeffrey, Mindy, and Zach for the experience of seeing their daddy's body, now bearded and so gaunt.

In tears, they all move to the casket and say their goodbyes. Gracia knows she will miss her husband terribly—most of all, perhaps, the laughter and twinkle in his eyes, the upbeat attitude that said "no problem is ever too tough to overcome, no ordeal too grim to endure."

Gracia places her hand on his chest. *Martin. You went through so much. You were so brave, and you kept me going so I could return home. I'll always love you.*

That night, after her children are asleep and Gracia is alone, she reflects on her incredible loss and her amazing husband. She is so sad Martin is gone—and so glad that his ordeal has ended and that he's in the presence of Jesus, the Lord he served with gladness until his final breath.

Would You? Could You?

(Share your answers if you're reading in a group)

For more than a year of captivity in the jungle, Martin Burnham was able to demonstrate an attitude of Christian love—not only to his wife and fellow hostages, but also to the kidnappers who held him. He told his wife, "Jesus said that if you want to be great in God's kingdom, be the servant of all. And when he said all, he meant all. He didn't say be the servant of everyone but terrorists."

Gracia Burnham admits that she sometimes struggled with such ideas. She knew, for instance, that she should have been able to forgive her captors. "The truth is that I often hated them," she says. "I despised them not only for snatching me away from my family and the simple comforts of a life I loved, but also for forcing me to see a side of myself I didn't like . . . fearful Gracia, selfish Gracia, bitter Gracia, angry-at-God Gracia. That wasn't the only me, but it was a bigger part of me than I wanted to accept." Gracia discovered what she called "pockets of darkness" inside her.

So what's inside of you? When the superficial layers we all carry around with us are stripped away, what's left— overflowing love and goodness or ugly fear and anger? At the core, are you a servant or are you selfish? If you don't know, maybe your next crisis will help you find out.

- What if you were kidnapped by terrorists—*could you* serve and even love them the way Martin Burnham apparently did? *Would you* follow the example of the Burnhams and pray for them daily?
- Gracia says she struggled with bitterness and hate. Would *you* if you were in her shoes? Have you hated someone before? Why?
- By the time Gracia met with Philippine President Gloria Macapagal Arroyo, she had let go of the anger and bitterness she felt about the way her rescue was handled. *Could you* do the same? Why or why not?
- Martin was a "servant of all" in small ways—by encouraging his wife, by repairing the terrorists' satellite phone, by carrying heavy loads without complaint. Are

our small acts of service just as important as our big ones? Do you serve this way when you're under stress?

- Jesus Christ washed the feet of his disciples and said, "I have set you an example that you should do as I have done for you" (John 13:15). He also said, "The Son of Man did not come to be served but to serve, and to give his life" (Matt. 20:28). How important is service in the life of a Christian?

- Muslim extremists rely on force, kidnapping, and murder to advance their cause. Gracia Burnham has written that Christians must defuse their rage and resentment through God's love. "People in today's world, whether Muslim or not, will not pay attention to Christians because we can explain our theology in crystal-clear terms," she says. "They will not esteem us because we give to charity or maintain a positive outlook on life. What will impress them is genuine love in our hearts." How can we demonstrate this love?

Reporting In

Ask the Lord to show you what is most in your heart, a spirit of servanthood or a spirit of selfishness. Then pray for him to show you how to serve him by serving others.

Hitting the Trail

(This is just for you)

You could say that Jesus Christ was a rebel. He challenged the existing order and long-held assumptions about faith and allegiance. He changed the world and inspired an ever-expanding "army" of followers—not through violence but through love.

We don't know for certain that Martin Burnham's servant attitude had an impact on the Abu Sayyaf terrorists, but we can speculate that his loving example influenced everyone who knew him well. What effect are you having on the people around you?

- List acts of service and love you've performed in the last week, whether grand or seemingly insignificant. How is your behavior challenging and changing the people in your world?

  _____

  _____

  _____

  _____

- Who serves and loves you? How do they show it? How do you respond to their actions?

  _____

  _____

  _____

- What would happen if you ramped up your commitment to serving others? Write down what you imagine would change, both in others' lives and in your own. Then pray about the idea of making it happen.

  _____

  _____

  _____

New Territory

(For those who want to explore further)

Read *In the Presence of My Enemies*, Gracia Burnham's account of her and Martin's year of terror in the jungle, and

To Fly Again, Gracia's thoughts on the spiritual lessons she's absorbed since her captivity and release.

- In what ways would your response to kidnapping and the loss of a spouse have been the same as Gracia's? How do you think your response would have been different?
- Did God use these tragic events for good in Gracia's life? In the lives of others?

PART THREE

PERSEVERANCE

9

Sailing the World at Seventeen

Difficult things take a long time,
impossible things a little longer.

Author unknown

For the past several hours, the sea has been kind to Zac Sunderland. He's been cruising along in a steady wind of eight knots, remembering the amazing sight of dolphins surfing in his wake the day before and reflecting on how good the recent R & R was in Darwin, Australia—for both him and his faithful sailboat *Intrepid*. Today the swells have picked up. He's sitting in the cockpit, enjoying the sensation of riding up and down the waves like a giant surfer.

It's October 4, 2008, about 150 miles off the coast of Indonesia. Zac is a month shy of his seventeenth birthday and more than fifteen hundred miles from his home in Thousand Oaks, California. He's trying to achieve a dream—to become the youngest person ever to sail solo around the world.

As he "surfs," Zac glimpses a boat about four miles away. He looks at his radar screen to check its course, but to his surprise the boat doesn't show up there. It appears they'll pass each other with plenty of room to spare. Still, he goes below to try to contact the other vessel on his VHF radio. There's no response. On a whim, he grabs his video camera and pops back up to shoot footage of the boat.

Suddenly, the boat changes course. It's heading directly for *Intrepid*.

Zac drops the video camera and adjusts his autopilot to change his own course, but the boat swerves again and speeds up, zeroing in on him. Zac sees now that it's a beat-up, sixty-foot powerboat, nothing like the usual commercial vessels traveling that route to Australia.

I've got a ship with no flags and no radio response that doesn't show up on radar, and it's deliberately heading straight for me, he thinks.

He comes to a frightening conclusion: *pirates*.

Zac, the oldest child of a boatbuilder, virtually grew up on the water. He spent many of his early years in vessels off the Mexican coast. He learned to refurbish dinghies and sail yachts. He was so skilled and comfortable on the water that when he approached his parents with the idea of sailing alone around the world, they agreed. His mother said at the time, "He's been training for this his entire life without knowing it."

But none of Zac's training has prepared him for an armed attack by sea raiders. He turns on *Intrepid*'s engine, slams it into gear, jumps back down into the cabin, and switches on the high frequency radio that transmits his position on all emergency channels.

The unidentified boat is still coming.

It's time to call home.

Zac turns on his satellite phone and is dismayed when the display screen flashes "low battery." Moving quickly, he plugs it into the charger and punches in the familiar number.

Laurence and Marianne Sunderland and their other six children are just sitting down to dinner when the portable phone rings. One of Zac's sisters answers. Laurence can hear his son's shout from where he's sitting. He grabs the receiver, rushes into another room, and listens carefully as Zac explains the crisis.

Laurence instructs his son to load the .357-caliber pistol he's carrying on the boat, then broadcast his situation and position on the emergency radio channel.

Laurence hates what he has to say next: "If they have guns and they're coming to do you harm, you're going to have to shoot to kill. Otherwise you will be killed."

Zac hangs up the phone, jams bullets into his pistol, and watches through *Intrepid*'s bulletproof windows as the powerboat moves closer—too close. He adjusts the autopilot again and kicks the engine up to maximum RPMs. *Intrepid* and the powerboat pass each other.

While Zac keeps motoring away, the powerboat stops dead in *Intrepid*'s wake. Zac keeps an eye on it. The powerboat sits in position, silent, for ten long minutes. Suddenly, its engine revs and it speeds away in the opposite direction.

The immediate danger is over, but Zac spends a sleepless night wondering if his "friends" will return. They don't. It's just another adventure on the journey of a lifetime.

In many ways, Zac is a typical California teen. He's six feet tall, 165 pounds, and has long hair. He plays video games (he has Guitar Hero III on *Intrepid*), skateboards, and wears Tony Hawk T-shirts. But Zac also has dreams. A book of photos about Robin Lee Graham, an American who at age twenty became the youngest person to sail around the world, inspired Zac. When he approached his dad with the idea of sailing around the world, his father realized he was serious.

"Do you think I could do it?" Zac said.

"Yes, you probably could," his dad answered.

"Would you let me?"

"I'll have to talk to your mother. This is a pretty big thing."

Once he secured the okay from his parents, Zac worked and saved his money, eventually coming up with the six thousand dollars he needed to purchase *Intrepid*, a no frills, thirty-six-foot Islander sailboat built in 1972. For three months, Zac and his dad labored to outfit and upgrade the boat. Zac even painted flames under *Intrepid*'s waterline. In June 2008, the sixteen-year-old sailed away from California and into the Pacific with high hopes.

A month after the pirate scare, Zac's dream is being tested again. He's in the Indian Ocean, fighting squalls with ten-foot swells. Thirty-knot winds have somehow yanked his forestay free from the chain plate on the bow. Now they're whipping the suddenly useless genoa sail to and fro from the top of the mast. The storm howls above the repeated clang of the metal clamp against the hull. Zac knows if he can't get it under control, the mast could break. His adventure could be over—or worse.

Zac again calls his dad for advice, then works through the night on the treacherous deck trying to contain the forestay. A gust sends the flapping genoa flying out from the boat and whips the forestay back at Zac. He barely jumps out of the way in time; only his safety harness saves him from falling overboard.

Exhausted and almost delirious, Zac finally rigs a kind of lasso, catches the end of the forestay, and stabilizes it until he can do a better job in the daylight. Later, he sails his crippled boat into port at Rodrigues Island in the middle of the Indian Ocean. There he obtains what he needs most—repairs and a good night's sleep.

Months later, Zac faces a different obstacle. He's on his way to the island of St. Helena, Napoleon's final resting place, but the winds have died and there's something wrong with the starter on his engine. Zac is adrift in the doldrums of the South Atlantic and bored out of his mind.

Out of frustration, Zac bangs his head on the cabin's low ceiling and pounds a dent into the top of his microwave with his fist. Finally, he draws down his sails, ties a rope around his waist, and jumps into the sea for a swim. It's a risk he probably wouldn't have taken at the beginning of his voyage. Today, it feels like a necessity.

That night, the wind picks up enough for Zac to begin sailing again. He reaches St. Helena a few days later and repairs the engine.

By the end of April, Zac is almost in the home stretch. He's approaching Grenada, a planned stopover before going through the Panama Canal and back into the Pacific.

Zac is tired. His radar has stopped working, and without its warning beeps, he has to wake up every twenty minutes to check for nearby ships. After a call home, he slides his satellite phone into a secure drawer in the cabin but forgets to turn it off.

Up on deck for one of his many middle-of-the-night vigils, he notices that one of the lines on the port side has chafed through and is trailing along in the water. He clips on his safety harness and reaches to pull in the line. His dad taught him that sailing is 80 percent hard work and 20 percent bliss. Zac realizes his father was right. But for just a moment on this night, the work and the bliss merge into a single experience. As he leans over the water in the pitch blackness, Zac sees something in *Intrepid*'s wake that few men ever view: the eerie, green, phosphorescent glow emitted by phytoplankton, the same glow that can create a kind of residual "daylight" in the ocean's great depths. Zac is spellbound as he pulls in the line.

Suddenly, he hears an all-too-familiar roar. He looks up just in time to see a thirty-foot rogue wave, speckled with the glowing phosphorescence, about to break over him.

Zac hugs the mast with all his strength. The wave slams onto the deck, covering it with water. Zac barely hangs on.

A few moments later, down in the cockpit, he sees the real damage—the inside of the boat is soaked. He quickly flips off switches on the drenched electrical panel, but it's too late. There is a flash of sparks and fire . . . and then just smoke.

115

There will be no more AC power until repairs in Grenada. No way to send emails or to charge his satellite phone, which is now useless with a drained battery.

Back home, Laurence and Marianne grow more concerned than they've ever been during Zac's test of endurance. The communication blackout comes at the end of the longest leg of his voyage—nearly five weeks alone on the Atlantic. They know the danger for the most alert of sailors, let alone someone as fatigued as Zac must be. Laurence flies to Grenada for what he'd previously hoped would be a routine visit with Zac.

Finally, in Grenada, Laurence spots *Intrepid*'s sail on the horizon. From a speedboat, he greets his son.

"How do you feel, Zac?" he calls out.

"I'm really, really tired."

Laurence shows him where to dock. For the next few days, Zac stays busy with eating, sleeping, boat maintenance, and media interviews. His dad and others work long, hard days as they check off the major repairs needed before they can wave happily and see Zac off again.

The seas take one more shot at Zac on the final leg of his journey up the coast of Mexico. A huge wave launches *Intrepid* out of the water and slams her down with a crack like the report of a high-powered rifle. Zac discovers that the thick teak bulkhead has snapped, a potentially catastrophic situation with Hurricane Andre brewing off the coast. He's forced to limp once again into an unplanned port, Banderas Bay near Puerto Vallarta, for his most significant repairs yet.

Once again, Laurence's boat-building skills are needed. He meets Zac at the marina, where he discovers he must remove the entire bulkhead, which also means removing the headliner and cabinets and cutting into the interior molded glass. Finally, however, the repairs are complete.

Dad and crew, and some members of the press, follow Zac's small but mighty *Intrepid* back out to sea in a spectacular 130-foot yacht that says it all with a very long and loud hoot on its air horn. Zac's tiny sail aims once again for the horizon.

Zac's next blog entry also says a lot: "Last night I passed the prison islands called the Tres Marias, and now I am tacking my way toward Baja. *Intrepid* feels strong and ready for the ride. I am so grateful for all the prayers and to my dad who has been an absolute hero."

When his mom emails him that they're planning a hero's welcome on his return, he replies, "Why? I'm just sailing."

On July 16, 2009, Zac "just sails" into Marina Del Rey, California, where his twenty-eight-thousand-mile journey began. His dream is fulfilled—he's made it and broken the solo circumnavigation record. On the way in, he's surrounded by pleasure boats, a coast guard vessel, a sheriff's department boat, and at least three helicopters.

After greeting family and friends, Zac steps to a podium and addresses a crowd of media and well-wishers. He tells them that society shouldn't put young people in a box. "There's so much more potential that people can do with the right motivation and the right ambition in life, so, you know, my thing would just be to get out there and do hard things. Go for it."

Zac expects to follow his own advice. He says he'll spend some time doing interviews and recovering from the voyage. But he doesn't plan on staying home too long. He's already thinking about his next adventure.

Would You? Could You?

(Share your answers if you're reading in a group)

Laurence and Marianne Sunderland have been criticized for allowing their son to risk his life to chase dreams on the high seas. Some point to scientific evidence that shows many teens struggle with evaluating risk. "Teenagers are still in the midst of a dynamic period in their brain development and their ability to make decisions," says Dr. Elisabeth Guthrie, a pediatrician and psychiatrist at New York's Columbia University. "In general, teenagers are nowhere near as mature in their decision-making abilities as adults. Teenagers do, in general, believe that they're much more immortal than they actually are, so they're not necessarily good at assessing how a particular risk may pertain to them."

Others say the decision depends on the teen. "When calculating a risk, it's important to take into account who you are and what you know," says Barbara McRae, parenting expert and founder of Teenfrontier.com. "He's been a sailor since childhood and was essentially born on a boat. I'd say Zac is ready to live his dream. If it were a situation where somebody was not prepared and was not passionate, I'd say absolutely not. I don't think the [Sunderland parents] are being bad parents—they're supporting their son with his dreams and not allowing their fear to get in the way of that."

Risk. Maturity. Growth. Experience. The ability to persevere. The unknowns of a round-the-world voyage. The list of considerations is endless. So where's *your* bottom line?

- Assuming you had the technical skill, *could you* handle a round-the-world sailing voyage—alone? *Would you* take on the challenge?
- How do you respond to this statement by Marianne Sunderland: "There are risks, but we look straight at them and minimize them and feel that it's not negligent by any means. I obviously don't want him to die, but I would not have any second doubts. If [he died] it would be devastating, but you can't live life ruled by fear."
- What are the ideal character qualities of an individual who plans to spend a year alone at sea?
- Zac's website says that "with perseverance and faith in God, anything is possible." Do you agree with this statement? What role does faith in God play in taking on a long-term challenge?
- The apostle Paul wrote, "We know that suffering produces perseverance; perseverance, character; and character, hope" (Rom. 5:3–4). Does extreme adventure require

or produce perseverance—or both? Paul seems to say that suffering eventually leads to hope—but hope in what?

• When Zac first proposed his idea of a solo circumnavigation, Marianne Sunderland said, "He's been training for this his entire life without knowing it." What might you be training for today without knowing it? What do you wish you were preparing for?

Reporting In

Are you willing to suffer or endure a long-term challenge in order to acquire perseverance, character, and hope? Pray about it.

Hitting the Trail

(This is just for you)

If you haven't embarked on any long ocean voyages lately, it may be time to ratchet up your suffering and perseverance quotient—not because you enjoy pain, but because it can lead to character, hope, and a deeper faith. Let's get into it.

• Write down what "extreme adventure" means to you. It might be a thirty-mile hike, a hundred-mile bike ride, a glider flight, a kayak trip down the rapids, a motorcycle tour, a summit attempt—or, if your mind and body are more accustomed to licorice and late nights surfing the internet, maybe it's a jog around the park. Choose whatever it is that sounds exciting and will stretch you, and write down a plan here for making it happen.

_____

_____

_____

- Make a list of goals for your adventure. Whether they are deepening your relationship with the Lord, taking time for praise and worship, or simply admiring his creation, be sure to include God in your reckoning.

  _____

  _____

  _____

- Do you know anyone who has developed a strong ability to persevere? Corner those people and ask them about their secrets.

  _____

  _____

  _____

New Territory

(For those who want to explore further)

Read *A Voyage for Madmen*, the bestseller by Peter Nichols about the 1968 Golden Globe round-the-world sailing race. Watch the documentary *Deep Water*, an exploration of the tragic saga of Donald Crowhurst, a competitor in the Golden Globe race. Read *Dove* and watch the movie *The Dove*, which tell the story of Robin Lee Graham's five-year voyage around the world that began in 1965.

- Of the nine participants in the round-the-world contest, whom do you admire the most? The least? Why? Which one most reminds you of you?
- Has your opinion changed about taking on the risk of a solo circumnavigation? Why or why not?

10

Cold Night in the Elk Mountains

We consider blessed those who have persevered.

James 5:11

At the start, I didn't think a bit about hypothermia or desperate thirst or whether I'd see my wife again. I was with friends on an adventure. That was what mattered.

It was all Dick Savidge's idea. He'd called me a couple of weeks before at my office in Glendora, California. "Peb!" he'd said. "Let's go get scared." Dick and I had been partners in crime before: ice climbs and a summit of the Petit Grepon in Rocky Mountain National Park; adventures with Tim Hansel's Summit Expedition outfit; and ice climbs in Vail, including the day Dick broke his leg on the treacherous Rigid Designator. The idea this time was to cross-country ski through twenty miles of snow country over a pass into Aspen. Dick knew I was ready for any chance to test my limits.

That's how we found ourselves standing at a trailhead near Crested Butte, Colorado, on a January morning in 1989: Dick, a former Outward Bound instructor from Denver; Stevan Strain, a restaurant owner and Himalayan climber from Colorado Springs; Bill, a Colorado carpenter and alpine-style climber; and me, Peb Jackson, an outdoorsman who was always looking for an excuse to return to the elements. It was 4 a.m. The night was bold and black, the stars intense from our vantage point at about eight thousand feet. It was also twenty degrees below zero, a "snap, crackle, and pop" cold.

Our intention was to cross-country ski to another trailhead in Aspen, more than twenty miles northeast as the crow flies. The terrain was difficult, a series of passes and ridges and slopes. We'd never heard of anyone making the journey in a single day. But we were all in great shape and confident of our abilities in the outdoors—maybe too confident. We wore insulated long underwear and several layers of clothing but carried no tents or sleeping bags, no down of any kind. We had no stove. Our food supply consisted of energy bars and water bottles. The plan was to travel light and fast and arrive in Aspen by dark.

That was the plan.

I was enthralled during those first hours. Despite having to break trail through heavy snow, we made good progress along an old jeep trail. The only sounds were of ice and twigs crackling beneath our skis and our own breathing. The crisp air froze inside my nose and throat. Even in the extreme cold, I quickly worked up a sweat.

A couple of hours into the journey, the first hints of a gorgeous sunrise appeared over the top of the Elk Mountains ahead of us. It was an amazing sight: a blanket of pristine snow, endless spires of evergreen trees that cast long black shadows, and an overcoat of orange rays draped across the landscape. We were surrounded by stark beauty.

"Dick," I huffed as we hiked, "we've been a lot of places together. I love this environment. It's primal territory."

"Peb, that's exactly why I call you," Dick replied. "You're always game."

It was midmorning when we reached a small wooden sign etched with the words "Pearl Pass" and an arrow pointing left.

This was the landmark we were looking for. We consulted our crude map to confirm our bearings, but its lack of detail provided little help. We turned in the direction of the arrow and pushed on, continuing to sink with our skis into heavy powder past our knees with each step.

Only later did we learn our mistake. Pearl Pass was actually dead ahead. Something or someone had turned the sign. We were heading into unknown territory.

A couple of hours later, Stevan was breaking trail, and I was second in line. Stevan glanced over his shoulder at me and without stopping said, "You know, something's not quite right here. We should be at the pass by now."

"You're right," I said. "But we'll get out of here." I knew that once we got over Pearl Pass, it was a straight shot to Aspen. Yet for the first time, I felt a tug of concern. As the sun dropped lower in the sky, my concern grew.

It was late afternoon when we reached the upper end of a cirque. Beyond it was the top of what we thought was Pearl Pass. This steep gulley, however, was not a place we wanted to be. It looked ripe for an avalanche. Yet to go higher was impossible; it was too steep. Turning around was equally unappealing. We were twelve hours and many miles into the journey. We also knew that Dick's wife was waiting alone for us at the Aspen trailhead. In these days before cell phones, we had no way of contacting her.

We gathered in a small huddle. Despite the subzero temperature, I was hot from the exertion and terribly thirsty. I pulled a water bottle from inside my jacket, where I'd placed it long before in hopes of melting it. No luck—the water was still frozen. Next I tried an energy bar. It too was frozen, but I was able to bite off a small piece to chew.

We weighed the alternatives. "I still don't know exactly where the heck we are," Stevan said, "but I've got to believe that if we can get across this slope and over the pass, the hike to Aspen shouldn't be too bad."

Bill looked behind us. "I don't want to go back now," he said. "We'd be hiking all night." He surveyed the slope in front of us, then turned to Dick and me. "What do you guys think? It looks a little dicey, but we don't have much choice. Are you up for moving ahead?"

According to the Colorado Avalanche Information Center, avalanches kill about twenty-five people in the United States each year, including six per annum in Colorado. The most dangerous are slab avalanches, which occur when stronger snow overlies weaker snow. A single man disturbing this perilous terrain is enough to ignite a massive shift in the landscape. In seconds, a slope as long as half a football field can simply disappear.

"We've got to do this," Dick said. "But we've got to be really careful."

I took a deep breath. I also took consolation in knowing these guys were experienced climbers. I trusted their judgment.

"Let's get going," I said. "I'm getting cold."

The field in front of us was about a hundred yards across and far too steep for us to stop ourselves if we fell, especially without ice axes. Below it was a drop of several hundred feet. It might as well have been ten thousand.

Stevan would go first. He took off his skis and strapped them on his back. He would kick steps across the slope, using his poles for balance as he moved. There was no point in roping up—if one of us fell, he'd take the rest with him. Stevan began gingerly picking his way across the slope while the rest of us held our breath.

Less than an hour later, Stevan and Dick were safely across. It was my turn. *Lord*, I prayed, *give me energy. Keep me safe. Help me to keep my focus.* I stepped onto the slope and felt the snow compact beneath my boots. I was grateful that Stevan had kicked in a trail. I tried to will myself to be as light as possible.

A couple years earlier, I'd been crossing a similar stretch of snow at the Maroon Bells near Aspen. I was about twenty yards into the slope, carefully checking each step but trying to move at a steady pace, when a friend behind me called out, "Peb, don't even think about it. Just go." I heard the urgency in his voice. What he wasn't telling me was that a crack in the snow had just opened up behind me. Thankfully, that one didn't develop into a slab avalanche. I'm not sure to this day why it didn't.

This time, I didn't waste energy looking around. I kept my eyes straight ahead and focused on making progress. I couldn't afford to let my mind drift. This was the ultimate moment for paying close attention. I gave myself to the rhythm of it—step to the right, place the pole, adjust for balance, breathe. Do it all again.

It felt as if time stood still.

Yet with each step and breath, time did pass. Twenty minutes later, I was across.

By the time Bill joined us, it was nearly dark. Grateful to still be alive and together, we climbed up the rocky incline that led to a ridge. Finally, after some thirteen hours of hiking, we reached the top of a pass—though not the one we were looking for. From Pearl Pass, we would have seen the lights of cabins. Here, there was nothing ahead of us but blackness. Only later did we learn it was Triangle Pass, thirteen thousand feet above sea level and at least two miles to the west of our intended goal.

I remembered the time that Dick and I thought we were climbing the Petit Grepon until we realized the route was much tougher than we anticipated. Somehow we'd gotten on the wrong face. We'd had to rappel off in the rain—Dick fell once—then hike out for seven miles.

How do we get into these things? I wondered.

We put on skis again and in the darkness picked our way through rocks and steep grades. At one point, Bill's binding broke. We had to jury-rig a repair job.

I was exhausted and dehydrated. I hadn't had a drink since early in our trek. I felt a hot spot at the bottom of my right foot, but didn't realize then that my sock was filling with blood where my skin had rubbed raw against the heel of my boot.

We'd already taken one wrong turn. In the back of my mind, I acknowledged a growing awareness of the consequences if we made another wrong decision. We couldn't stop because we didn't have the gear to survive a night in these conditions. I was grateful to be going downhill after so many hours going up, but I was also feeling wasted.

I knew that the secret to covering a long distance was to focus on small objectives. On the way up, I'd thought, *I'll just get to that next boulder. It's only a hundred yards.* One step at a time, we were creating a mosaic in the snow, small strips of trail that would form what we hoped was our deliverance.

We each wore headlamps that brought small comfort in the deepening darkness. For the next two hours, we skied close together and focused on avoiding rocks. A broken ankle here would be seriously bad news. I concentrated on trying to stay upright.

Suddenly, Bill's voice cut through the night: "You guys smell something?"

I sniffed. "Smells like smoke," I said, improbable as that sounded.

A minute later, I could make out a black mass roughly thirty yards away and illuminated by flickering light from within. How could something be on fire out here? As we approached, I could see that it was a broken-down miner's cabin.

With newfound hope, we hurried to the "door" of the tiny cabin—an old rug hanging over the opening—and peeked inside. To our amazement, a man and woman were sitting there in sleeping bags. They were brewing up a small pot of tea and huddled close to a couple of logs burning in a fire pit.

"Mind if we join you?" Stevan asked.

The couple looked so startled that words failed them for a moment. "Where did you guys come from?" the woman finally said.

"Crested Butte."

"You're kidding."

We stumbled into the small space and stood there with silly grins on our faces. The joy of that moment is impossible to relate. To find an oasis and human contact in this primitive place was a gift beyond what we'd hoped for.

Still, our relief was tempered by the news that we were a good six miles from Aspen, and we had to push on. Even if we'd had a way to stay warm overnight, there wasn't room for six of us here. We enjoyed a few sips of tea, the first liquid to reach our parched lips for many hours, and chewed on a few bites of granola. Then we slipped on our skis and stepped back into the dark woods. It all happened so quickly that it didn't seem real.

Even though we were going downhill, it still required maximum effort. My legs felt like sticks. I knew I didn't have much left. I concentrated on keeping a rhythm: *Left. Right. Breathe.*

A couple of hours later, Dick's voice broke the stillness of the night: "Look."

I glanced up. Perhaps a mile distant were a few yellow pinpricks. They were the lights of cabins. It meant people, civilization, and rest were not far away.

Those lights were like a beacon during the final stage of our arduous journey. I recalled the words of John about Christ: "What came into existence was Life, and the Life was Light to live by. The Life-Light blazed out of the darkness; the darkness couldn't put it out" (John 1:4–5 Message).

It was probably after midnight, more than twenty hours since our departure, when we dragged ourselves to the front door of one of the cabins on the outskirts of Aspen. We would have been a frightening sight—four exhausted men, icicles hanging from our beards, barely able to stand up. But we didn't care. We'd made it.

When a man opened the door, we all stared at each other for a few moments. In a raspy, barely audible voice, I finally got out the words that needed to be said.

"Would you please call for a taxi?"

Would You? Could You?

(Share your answers if you're reading in a group)
"Alpine style" is a mountaineering term for the idea of bringing what is necessary and nothing more—traveling light and fast to the summit. It means less exposure to the risks of avalanche and weather, but also less margin for error. Herman Buhl was among the first to employ these tactics on high peaks in the 1950s. Two decades later, Reinhold Messner and Peter Habeler popularized the style, starting with the summit of the Himalayan peak Gasherbrum I in 1975. Messner eventually became the first man to summit Everest without supplemental oxygen in 1978.

This was the approach our (Peb's) team had in mind when we set out for Aspen that cold day in 1989. We were confident in our outdoor skills. By foregoing overnight gear, we planned to move quickly and arrive in Aspen by nightfall. The problem, of course, was that our wrong turn left us vulnerable to nature's icy grip. In retrospect, a stove would have been nice!

For some of us, alpine style is more than a method of climbing or cross-country skiing. It's a way of life. We set aside precautions others cling to and push hard and fast for the goal. It's a thrilling existence, one that frequently leads to the razor-thin edge between success and disaster.

How close to the edge are *you* willing to go to achieve your goals?

- *Would you* put yourself at risk to ski without overnight gear across the Elk Mountains, as these men did? *Could you* have persevered when it became obvious the plan had gone awry?
- Should they have turned around at the avalanche field?
- What level of risk should people strive for in outdoor pursuits: Low? Medium? High? What about in business?

How about other areas of life such as relationships and family?

- How can we tell the difference between a foolhardy risk and one that is going to help us grow?

- Dick Savidge's invitation to the Aspen adventure began with the line, "Let's go get scared." Why are so many of us attracted to the idea of being scared? Is this healthy or not? Does it help us value the gift of life? Does it help us understand the Bible's admonition to "Fear the LORD your God" (Deut. 6:13)?

- Peb said that "the secret to covering a long distance was to focus on small objectives." Is this true in all aspects of life? What are some examples?

- When we persevere in other areas of life, does this also strengthen our ability to persevere in faith and service to the Lord?

Reporting In

Scripture says, "We consider blessed those who have persevered" (James 5:11). Are you persevering in your faith through hard times or difficult journeys? Thank the Lord for his blessing and ask him for guidance and strength.

Hitting the Trail

(This is just for you)

The life of faith is a daring adventure, full of risk and danger. Jesus said, "Risk your life and get more than you ever dreamed of. Play it safe and end up holding the bag" (Luke 19:26 Message). The problem is that many of us *are* playing it safe. We rest in our comfortable routine, never asking the Lord if he wants more of us.

Let's take a closer look at the purpose and meaning of risk.

- Make two lists—one of potential benefits to taking risks and the other of potential drawbacks. Include examples from your life.

  _____

  _____

  _____

  _____

- Write down examples from Scripture of people who took risks for their faith. Now add people you know personally to the list. Does your name belong on the list?

  _____

  _____

  _____

  _____

- Write down any risks that the Lord might be asking you to consider today. What is holding you back from moving ahead? Pray about it.

  _____

  _____

  _____

New Territory

(For those who want to explore further)

Read *The Worst Journey in the World*, Apsley Cherry-Garrard's retelling of Robert Scott's doomed expedition to the South Pole, and *The Crystal Horizon*, Reinhold Messner's account of the first solo ascent of Everest.

- What enabled Scott and Messner to persevere despite incredible obstacles? Did their goals (especially considering the deaths of Scott and his men) justify the risk?
- How would you describe the quality and character of these men? Are these qualities admirable or something to be avoided? Why?

11

The Miracle Girl

Sorrow and silence are strong, and
patient endurance is godlike.

Henry Wadsworth Longfellow

Her vision is blurred. For the fifth—or is it *sixth*?—day
since Christmas, she picks her way over fallen trees
and huge rocks along a riverbank in the Amazon
jungle. The frilly miniskirt she wore to her high school graduation is ripped, and her white high heels are left behind in
the mud. Thorns tear at her feet. Her glasses are gone; one
eye is swollen shut. The pain she feels in her shoulder with
every step is from a broken collarbone.

She sleeps fitfully at night as jaguars creep by, crocodiles
slide into the water, and unknown insects crawl over her legs.
But her greatest fear is from the maggots that have burrowed
into the festering wound in her arm and are now wriggling
under her skin and eating into her flesh.

She wonders if her arm will have to be amputated.

If she survives.

Only a few days earlier, it was Christmas Eve 1971, and seventeen-year-old Juliane Koepcke was looking forward to the upcoming airplane trip. She'd always had more faith in planes than her mother, who never liked to fly. Her parents were both well-known zoologists—her mother, Marie, at the Lima Museum and her father, Hans, studying wildlife at a research station in the jungle. LANSA Airlines in Peru had a bad reputation after two previous crashes, and just two months ago an air force plane from Uruguay had disappeared in the Andes while transporting a rugby team to Chile. But Juliane and Marie desperately wanted to be with Hans for Christmas.

So Juliane and her mother boarded the Lockheed Electra turboprop along with ninety other passengers for the one-hour trip from Lima to Pucallpa in the middle of the Amazon rainforest. Juliane took the window seat in the third row from the back on the right side. Marie sat next to her. They talked excitedly about their plans for the holiday.

The sky was sunny and clear as the plane took off. During the first twenty-five minutes of what seemed a routine flight, Marie became quiet and nervous. But Juliane happily watched the snow-covered Andes mountains pass below and then give way to the beautiful, endless jungle.

Suddenly, the plane was engulfed by dark clouds. The ride turned bumpy. Passengers were told to fasten their seat belts. Marie was petrified, but Juliane thought, *Strong winds are common over the mountains.* She held her mother's hand when pelting rain and lightning appeared.

Then the plane shook violently. Luggage and Christmas presents flew from the storage racks. People started to scream.

Another bolt of lightning flashed—much too close. Juliane saw bright yellow flames shoot out of the wing. The plane went into a nosedive.

"I knew it!" Marie cried. "This is the end of everything!"

Just as Juliane turned to look at her mother, the plane broke into pieces with a loud crack. Shrieking passengers tumbled out into the storm.

Then all was suddenly silent. Juliane was outside the plane but still buckled into her row of three seats, which whirled down like a helicopter blade. The jungle trees two miles below looked like spinning cauliflowers. She couldn't catch her breath. She passed out.

Dizzy and disoriented, Juliane came to upside down in the pouring rain. She was still strapped into her row of seats, which had flipped over on the jungle floor. A clap of thunder brought back memories of the plane, but she still couldn't think clearly. The seats next to her were . . . empty.

My mother! Where is she? Did anybody else make it?

Juliane managed to unbuckle herself from the seat and peer into the dense jungle.

"Anyone here?"

She couldn't see any other survivors or wreckage. In shock and too weak to stand, she curled up under the seats and fell asleep to the sounds of rain, croaking frogs, and buzzing insects.

Juliane awoke on Christmas morning. The numbness of shock had worn off. Her body throbbed with pain. But she could walk.

I survived, so maybe my mother and others did too. I've got to try to find her.

"Hello! Hello! Is anybody out there?"

I can't stay here. Search planes aren't going to spot me in this thick jungle. I have to get out of here and find help.

Juliane's parents taught her to look for a river if she were ever lost in the jungle because it would lead her to an Indian settlement, hunters, or loggers. They also taught her that hungry mosquitoes and other teeming jungle insects are a bigger threat than the jaguars, anteaters, wild pigs, and crocodiles. She knew the large animals weren't likely to attack if she left them alone.

She found a stick and beat the ground in front of her to check for snakes, spiders, or ants as she stepped slowly and carefully through the undergrowth. The jungle was still spinning. She stopped often to rest.

Soon Juliane's heart leaped at the distant sound of a creek. She found it, drank the clear water, and followed it down a gorge until it widened into a stream. The stream cut a winding path through the jungle, often doubling back on itself.

I feel like I'm going in circles, she thought. But she knew that straying from the thorny bank of the stream would be certain death.

I wish I could wade in the stream. But her feet bled from cuts. The blood would attract piranhas.

A loud buzzing sound ahead drew her attention. It was a row of seats from the plane, upside down. Juliane went to investigate and was horrified to find three female bodies in the seats, buried headfirst into the ground from the impact. They were covered with flies.

She screamed. Then she wept.

Juliane wanted to get away, but the shoes on one of the bodies looked familiar—her mother's? She used a stick to knock a shoe off. The toes had nail polish—which her mother never used.

It's five or six days after the crash, and Juliane is still walking. She'd eaten a few bites of cake on the first day and found a bag of hard Christmas candy, which she'd saved for the journey. Now the candy is long gone. All she has in her stomach is the lifesaving freshwater from the stream. She sees exotic fruits now and then and longs to eat them, but she isn't sure which are poisonous. Same for the fat toads on the stream bank.

Juliane discovers that fly eggs have hatched in the open wound in her arm and maggots are burrowing under her skin. Flies in the Amazon produce maggots that don't stop with eating decaying flesh—they grow into worms that keep eating into living tissue. This combined with the hundred-degree heat makes Juliane increasingly weak. She feels she can't go on, yet she knows her only hope is to keep moving. The occasional sounds of search aircraft stopped days ago. She hears the hisses and grunts of vultures off to the side of her path.

The stream has become a river, and Juliane decides to take a risk she would not have taken earlier. She desperately needs relief from the heat and the help of the current to move her along. She's a child of scientists who taught her to value hard facts. Now, however, she takes a moment on the bank to pray that the piranhas will leave her alone. Then she wades in and starts swimming.

It's January 2, nine days after the crash. Starving and exhausted, Juliane has willed herself to keep walking, swimming, or wading, but now the river's current is too swift. Up on the bank, a wide column of army ants blocks her path. In her weakened state, she is forced to detour around them. A single colony can turn an unconscious human into a skeleton within hours.

Suddenly, around one of the river bends, she sees it—a canoe pulled up on a little beach.

Finally, someone who can help me!

She follows a path through the jungle to a little shack, but nobody's there. It appears to have been deserted for weeks, maybe even months. She decides to rest in the shelter, where she can at least stay dry. But she must do *something* about the worms wriggling under the skin in her arm.

God, help me! They're eating me alive.

Using a sharp stick, she gouges out dozens of them, but can't get them all.

She falls asleep on the wooden floor and wakes the next morning to a heavy rain.

Will anyone return here in time?

She wonders if she should keep moving and considers taking the canoe but rejects the idea.

It would be stealing, and I'm too weak to handle it anyway.

So she lies down again to wait . . . or die. The patter of the rain and the cries of monkeys and parrots start to lull her to sleep when she hears another sound—men's voices! Three wet lumberjacks walk into the shack and cry out in surprise at their unexpected guest. Sobbing with relief, Juliane tells her story.

The men encourage her to eat what little they have, but the only thing she can think about is getting rid of the maggots. Drawing again on knowledge she gained from her father, she begs them to pour gasoline into her wound. When they do, dozens more of the worms come wriggling out.

After the men dress her wound and cover her with blankets and a mosquito net, they convince her it's too dark to move her until morning. The closest help the men can think of is an old Indian woman about two hours downriver. They will take her there by canoe in the morning.

Juliane is so glad for human companionship that she wants to talk more before falling asleep. One of the men tells her he was part of the search operation, but the heavy rains kept them from covering the area on foot. They hadn't been able to see any wreckage from the air.

Day ten. When the men and Juliane arrive at the Indian woman's hut, she takes one look at the teenager's swollen face and bloodshot eyes and shoos them off.

"Demon!" she shouts.

So they get back in the canoe and navigate the dangerous, swiftly flowing river another eight hours to the closest town, where Juliane finally gets medical care and is told her arm is going to be okay. A female American pilot flies her to a missionary camp near Pucallpa where she is hospitalized and reunited with her father.

Her information helps the searchers find the wreckage of the plane scattered over a ten-mile area. They discover that everyone else, including Juliane's mother, either died on impact or had perished in the jungle from their injuries.

A member of the search party observes, "Only God knows how that girl survived."

As Juliane recovers, she is labeled by the media as "The Miracle Girl." She receives hundreds of letters from strangers.

"It was so strange," she says years later. "Some of the letters were simply addressed 'Juliane—Peru,' but they still all found their way to me."

Like Juliane on her journey through the jungle, no matter how unlikely, some travelers seem meant to reach their destination.

Would You? Could You?

(Share your answers if you're reading in a group)

According to the would-be rescuers who searched the jungle after talking with Juliane Koepcke, a dozen people survived the crash of LANSA Airlines Flight 508 in the Amazon rainforest on Christmas Eve 1971. We can only speculate on why they remained where they were. Some probably thought that if they stayed with the wreckage, searchers would find them in time. Others may have felt that because of injuries sustained in the crash, they wouldn't get far. Perhaps some feared the unknown of the jungle more than starving to death. Whatever the reasons, it appears that only one survivor—seventeen-year-old Juliane—concluded that the canopy was too thick for anyone to see them from the air. Only Juliane made the decision that her survival depended on action.

Juliane had a survivor's mentality. She kept her cool. Even in the midst of her terrifying freefall, she had the presence of mind to note that the trees below looked like cauliflowers. On the ground, she foraged for food, avoided anything potentially poisonous, and remembered her parents' instructions to travel downriver. When she was starving and exhausted, she still pushed on. Though she lacked food, shelter, a lantern, an axe, matches, a compass, and any covering for her feet, she was nevertheless equipped intellectually and emotionally to face the greatest challenge of her life.

If survival is a test, the solution begins in the mind. There are no retakes. Are you ready to pass or fail?

- Let's say you've just lived through a plane crash into the jungle. *Would you* keep a clear head? *Could you* take the steps needed to save yourself? Where would you start?

- Besides what's described above, what else did Juliane do right after the crash? How might events have turned out very differently?

- Do you think Juliane was lucky, or is luck more about taking advantage of opportunities?

- As she recovered from her ordeal, some people told Juliane that God had blessed her. "But why me?" she asked. "And why not my mother?" How would you answer Juliane?

- In a recent interview, Juliane said she is not a spiritual person, yet in the jungle she prayed for protection from piranhas and later pored through the Bible searching for answers to her ordeal. Some would argue that our trials are more than coincidence and bad timing—that God allows trouble in our lives to draw us closer to him. Do you believe this is true?

- Jesus told his disciples that they "should always pray and not give up" (Luke 18:1). Does persevering in life help train us to persevere in prayer and faith? How about the other way around—does persistent prayer help us persevere in other areas?

Reporting In

Is God allowing you to face problems or even tragedy right now because he wants to teach you something about faith and perseverance? Ask him about it.

Hitting the Trail

(This is just for you)

Life is filled with unexpected challenges. Like Juliane Koepcke, someday we may suddenly be faced with choices that will mean the difference between life and death. Those moments in the crucible can be terrifying, but they can also teach us about ourselves and the nature of our faith in and relationship with God.

- Think about the hardest time in your life and how you responded to it. What got you through it? What did you learn from the experience? What do you wish you'd learned?

_____

_____

_____

- When you're faced with a challenge, do you turn to God and see him as part of the solution? Why or why not? Why would a good God allow us to suffer or face terrifying situations?

_____

_____

_____

• What can you do today to prepare yourself for an unexpected crisis? List your answers and include a timeline for accomplishing each.

_____

_____

_____

New Territory

(For those who want to explore further)

Watch the Werner Herzog documentary *Wings of Hope*, which takes Juliane Koepcke back to the jungle crash site seventeen years after her ordeal. Read *Desperate Journeys, Abandoned Souls* by Edward E. Leslie, which includes Juliane's story of survival along with many others. Also read *Miracle in the Andes*, Nando Parrado's account of his own struggle to survive after he and his Uruguayan rugby teammates crashed in the Andes Mountains in 1971.

• What do castaways and other survivors have in common? How are the survivors in *Desperate Journeys* and *Miracle in the Andes* unique?
• Who in your circle of friends and acquaintances is best equipped to be a survivor? Who is least equipped? Why?

12

To the Last Breath

You threw me into ocean's depths, into a watery grave,
with ocean waves, ocean breakers crashing over me.

Jonah 2:3 Message

John Chatterton is a diver. To earn a living, the forty-year-old with the Long Island accent works at underwater construction jobs in the Manhattan area. But his passion is shipwreck diving—the deeper and more daring, the better.

Many wreck divers are in the game only for "tonnage"—to fill their mesh goody bags with as many dishes, gear, and artifacts from a dead ship as they can. Chatterton has removed his share too, but for him it's about more than hauling up stuff. Diving is about exploration, about mapping the unknown. It's a chance to see what no one else has seen.

By the fall of 1991, few wrecks on America's eastern seaboard remain unexplored. So when a fishing boat captain gives Chatterton's mentor, diving legend Bill Nagle, the latitude and longitude of a site sixty miles off the New Jersey coast that promises to be "something big," Chatterton is quick to sign up for the dive. It's probably just a garbage barge or even a pile of rocks. But Chatterton has to find out.

On September 2, Nagle and thirteen men reach the mystery site aboard Nagle's dive boat, the *Seeker*. He and Chatterton examine the boat's electronic bottom finder. Something is there, but it's deeper than the men expected, about 230 feet below the surface. This is dangerous territory. No one has much experience at 230 feet.

Shipwreck divers face many risks. A broken pipe can cut an air hose. Loose cables can tangle up with oxygen tanks. And then there is nitrogen narcosis, every undersea explorer's nightmare. At depths greater than sixty-six feet, a diver's judgment and motor skills begin to falter. At more than one hundred feet below, the deterioration can be significant. Many a diver, confused by narcosis, has lost his way inside the twisting labyrinth that is the guts of a shipwreck. And the diver who stays too long cannot simply shoot for the surface. He must rise gradually, allowing the nitrogen he's accumulated from breathing gas to release into his bloodstream in tiny bubbles. If he surfaces too quickly, he risks the "bends"—large bubbles that form outside the bloodstream and block circulation. The result can be agonizing pain, paralysis, and death.

That's why, on the *Seeker*, the decision is that Chatterton will dive first, alone, to see if anything down there is worth the risk.

Chatterton splashes over the side. Six minutes later he lands on something hard. Even with his headlight, he can't see much at this depth—the water is a murky green and a snowstorm of white matter moves sideways around him. But he can make out patches of rust on metal and, above him, a curved railing and corner. He thinks it's a strange shape for what's probably a barge.

Chatterton moves slowly along the top of the wreck, careful to keep hold of it so the current doesn't carry him away. He comes to an open hatch and pokes his head and headlight inside.

144

It's a room. His light illuminates an object lying against one of the walls. The object is shaped like a cigar. It has fins and a propeller.

It isn't possible. Chatterton closes his eyes and opens them again.

The object is unmistakable. It's a torpedo.

I'm narced, Chatterton thinks. *I'm at 220 feet. I'm exhausted from fighting the current. I could be seeing things.*

You are on top of a submarine, another voice inside his brain replies.

There are no submarines anywhere near this part of the ocean. I have books. I have studied books. There are no submarines here. This is impossible.

You are on top of a submarine.

I'm narced.

There is no other shape like that torpedo. Remember those rolled edges you saw on the hull, the ones that looked built for gliding? Submarine. You have just discovered a submarine.

This is a huge dive.

No, John, this is more than a huge dive. This is the holy grail.

Chatterton recognizes from the deterioration of metal around him that the submarine must have sunk about a half-century ago. That places it during World War II. He also knows there are no sunken American submarines in the vicinity.

"I'm holding on to a U-boat," Chatterton says aloud. "I'm holding on to a World War II German U-boat."

As incredible as this realization is, finding the submarine isn't nearly as important to Chatterton as identifying it. It is part of his personal code, one he'd begun to develop as a boy, modeled in part by his grandfather. Rae Emmet Arison was a retired rear admiral who'd commanded submarines in the 1930s and led battleships in World War II. He was also a man who valued excellence and persistence.

Chatterton's code crystallized further during his service as a medic in the Vietnam War. He became known as a different kind of medic, one who risked everything to retrieve wounded and exposed soldiers, one who volunteered for patrols and often walked point. His experiences led him to identify a series of principles on the right way and wrong way to live.

The right way to live after discovering a U-boat is to identify it. For Chatterton, anything less is unacceptable.

That day in the ocean off the New Jersey coast becomes a defining moment in Chatterton's life. It is the beginning of a personal voyage to discovery and danger.

Some will call it a deadly obsession.

Two weeks after finding the submarine, almost all of the original thirteen divers return to the U-boat site. One is Steve Feldman, a stagehand at CBS television. Feldman and a buddy, excavation contractor Paul Skibinski, make their first dive of the day and penetrate a gaping hole in the sub's control room.

According to their conservative diving plan, after thirteen minutes inside, it's already time to go. Skibinski taps Feldman on the shoulder and points up. Feldman nods his okay. Skibinski turns and swims to the anchor line attached to the *Seeker*.

Skibinski looks behind him. Feldman has his back to Skibinski and seems to be checking out something on the wreck. Skibinski looks closer. No bubbles are rising from Feldman's regulator.

Something's not right, Skibinski thinks.

He swims over and turns his friend around.

Feldman's regulator falls from his mouth. He isn't blinking. He isn't breathing. He's gone.

Later, the divers speculate that Feldman simply blacked out, a not-uncommon occurrence at such depths.

Despite the tragedy, Chatterton, Nagle, and others—including dive-shop manager John Yurga and a new Chatterton ally, diver Richie Kohler—continue their quest to identify the sub. Chatterton flies to Chicago to study a U-boat at a museum. He communicates with U-boat experts in the United States and Germany. He pores over history books. Chatterton,

146

Yurga, and Kohler make trips to the Naval Historical Center and the National Archives and Records Administration in Washington, D.C. Chatterton and Yurga fly to Germany to investigate more possibilities.

As they research, one U-boat after another surfaces as the likely candidate to solve the puzzle. And as they dig deeper, each theory is shot down by new evidence. The mystery of what they start calling the "U-Who" deepens.

In October 1992, the men are back on the ocean in the *Seeker*, still searching for answers. This time the team includes Chris and Chrissy Rouse, a father-son tandem famous for their cave diving exploits.

On the first day, in the forward torpedo room, Chatterton snags a piece of aluminum. On deck, he discovers it's a schematic of a section of the U-boat. Inscribed along the edge are the words "Bauart IXC" and "Deschimag, Bremen." It's a revealing find—IXC is a type of U-boat and Deschimag, Bremen is a German shipyard. The information will narrow their search significantly.

On the second day of the trip, the weather turns nasty and promises to get worse. Only six of the fourteen divers decide to hit the water. Two of the six are the Rouses.

On a previous dive, Chrissy had found a piece of canvas with German writing on it in the galley, wedged under a tall steel cabinet. This time he returns to the galley, determined to free the canvas and discover its secrets. His father remains outside the wreck and shines a light for Chrissy to find on his return. The Rouses have twenty minutes.

For roughly fifteen minutes, Chrissy digs under the cabinet, sending silt everywhere. The canvas loosens, but not enough for it to be removed. Chrissy pulls with greater force. The canvas begins to come free—and so does the steel cabinet. It topples onto Chrissy, pinning him. He's trapped.

Outside the wreck, Chris Rouse can't see anything through the thick cloud of silt. But their time is up, and Chrissy is still in there. He swims into the galley, finds his son beneath the cabinet, and works to free him. Ten minutes later, both Rouses swim out of the galley. But the nylon line Chrissy extended into the galley is tangled from his struggle to escape. Narcosis further warps their judgment.

For their decompression, the Rouses had placed oxygen tanks forty feet aft of their entry point in the sub, near the anchor line to the *Seeker*. But now, disoriented and panicked, they swim in the wrong direction. The tanks are nowhere to be found. After forty minutes underwater and with little air left, both do the unthinkable—they forego decompression and shoot to the surface.

It is a fatal move. The bends kill Chris Rouse on board the *Seeker*. A Coast Guard helicopter rushes Chrissy to a New York hospital, where he dies a few hours later.

It's a devastating loss, but Chatterton won't stop now. One of his principles is that "the worst possible decision is to give up." He, along with Kohler and others, continues to research. The price of their quest grows ever higher. Late in 1993, Bill Nagle drinks himself to death. Both Chatterton's and Kohler's marriages collapse.

More theories on the identity of the sub are embraced and quashed. Then, in early 1994, comes a breakthrough. A British U-boat expert discovers that *U-869*, a German submarine believed to have been sunk off Gibraltar, may have never received its orders to proceed to the coast of North Africa. It may have continued on its original mission—to patrol American shores southeast of New York.

Further Chatterton research shows that the classification of *U-869*'s sinking off Gibraltar is shaky at best. But for Chatterton, a strong theory isn't enough. He has to know for certain.

Three more years of inconsequential dives and frustration pass. Chatterton and the rest have explored every room on the sub except one—the electric motor room. The problem is that the room is blocked by a heavy oil tank that's fallen in the diesel motor room. There's an opening just below the ceiling, but it's too small for a diver with oxygen tanks to wriggle through.

On August 31, 1997—almost six years to the day after finding the U-boat—Chatterton implements the final stage of a daring plan and swims into the diesel motor room. He's wearing one oxygen tank instead of two. Chatterton removes his lone source of air, pushes it and a sledgehammer through the opening that leads to the electric motor room, then slips through himself. He reattaches the oxygen tank.

The week before, Chatterton had entered the electric motor room the same way and videotaped a stack of boxes. He believes they are filled with spare parts that include tags that will conclusively identify the wreck. But the boxes are held in place by a heavy, five-foot section of pipe.

Chatterton swims deeper into the electric motor room and finds the boxes and pipe. He swings the sledgehammer, stirring up a cloud of rust particles. When the particles settle, Chatterton is dismayed. The pipe hasn't moved. And it's not a pipe at all. With the rust gone, he can see it's actually a pressurized oxygen tank. The sledgehammer blow could easily have triggered an explosion and killed him.

He has a decision to make.

When things are easy, a person doesn't really learn about himself, Chatterton thinks. *It's what a person does at the moment of his greatest struggle that shows him who he really is. Some people never get that moment.*

The U-Who is my moment. What I do now is what I am.

Chatterton lifts the sledgehammer and smashes it against the tank. Rust and silt again swirl about him, but there's no explosion—just the sound of metal against metal.

The cloud clears. The tank has fallen away.

Chatterton slips the smallest box, a bit bigger than a shoe box, into his mesh bag and swims out to the tiny opening in the diesel room. He pushes the box through to Kohler, who's accompanied him on the dive. Kohler passes it on to another diver who will send the box to the surface.

But Chatterton isn't finished. He's still got three minutes, time for another box.

149

The next box is bigger and heavier. Chatterton starts rolling it out. He realizes it's taking too much time. He's got to go.

Chatterton's efforts have stirred up the silt again. He's got no visibility. He swims up to navigate his way out along the ceiling. He's only a few feet away from the opening to freedom when something pulls him back by the neck. It's a wire hanging from the ceiling, looped around him.

He tries moving backward slowly. It makes things worse—the gear on his back also becomes entangled with cables.

Chatterton no longer has time to be careful. He rips the wire away from his throat. He struggles against the other cables once, then again. He's still trapped. He puts all his strength into the effort.

He's free. His oxygen tank is also down to its last breath of air.

Chatterton swims through the narrow opening near the ceiling, discards his oxygen tank, and pushes hard for his decompression oxygen bottles, located on top of the sub, forty feet away. He feels his lungs on the verge of bursting. It's going to be close.

Seconds later Chatterton finds the bottles, stuffs a regulator into his mouth, and turns a valve. He can breathe again. He's made it.

For nearly two hours, Chatterton silently decompresses with Kohler as they gradually move closer to the surface. The decompression is almost over when a diver swims down and hands Chatterton a slate with words written on it. They read:

The U-Who now has a name—it is *U-869*. Congratulations.

Would You? Could You?

(Share your answers if you're reading in a group)

Webster's dictionary defines *obsession* as "a persistent disturbing preoccupation with an often unreasonable idea or feeling." The lore of the sea is filled with examples of such compulsion, perhaps best illustrated by the fictional Captain Ahab in Melville's *Moby-Dick*. Like Ahab, John Chatterton was on a quest and would not be deterred. His motivation, however, was based more on a philosophy of life than on revenge.

Whether we recognize it or not, most of us are guided by a set of core beliefs that help direct our daily actions and decisions. Part of the adventure of living is discovering and embracing what we believe. Chatterton's beliefs on the right way to live led him to pursue the identification of the U-Who with single-minded intensity. He once told his wife, "I'm being tested. What I do with this U-boat is what I am as a person." Chatterton succeeded in the end, but he and others also paid dearly for the triumph.

How about it—do you have a "right way" to live? And how far are you willing to go to uphold your beliefs?

- If you were a skilled deep-sea diver and you'd found a mystery U-boat, *would you* feel compelled to identify it? *Could you* persevere when the going got tough?
- Do you respect John Chatterton for his efforts to identify *U-869* or do you think he was out of his mind—or both? Why?
- Is there ever a limit to how far a person should go in doing the right thing? Where is that line?
- Do you think Chatterton was being tested by his encounter with the U-boat? If so, did he pass the test?
- Do you agree with Chatterton's statement that what you do at the moment of your greatest struggle shows who you truly are?
- How important are excellence and persistence to your core beliefs?
- What should a person base his or her beliefs on: Experience? Logic? Faith? Why?
- The Bible says, "Love the LORD your God and keep his requirements, his decrees, his laws and his commands

always" (Deut. 11:1). Is this our guide to the right way to live? Why or why not?

Reporting In

Are you facing any tests of your commitment to excellence and perseverance today? If so, ask the Lord to show you how he wants you to handle them.

Hitting the Trail

(This is just for you)

John Chatterton's principles on life include statements like these: "If you follow in another's footsteps, you miss the problems really worth solving"; "Excellence is born of preparation, dedication, focus, and tenacity"; "It is easiest to live with a decision if it is based on an earnest sense of right and wrong."

Few of us take the trouble to write down the principles that we strive to live by. Now is your chance.

- Record here the central beliefs and principles that comprise the person you are (or wish to be). Take your time.

  _____

  _____

  _____

- Go through each item on your list. How are you illustrating (or failing to illustrate) each principle? List examples.

  _____

  _____

  _____

- What are the principles that Jesus Christ appeared to live by on earth? How do his principles compare with yours? What does this mean to you?

_____

_____

_____

New Territory

(For those who want to explore further)

Read _Shadow Divers_, Robert Kurson's bestselling tale of the quest to identify _U-869_, and watch _Hitler's Lost Sub_, the public television documentary about the same.

- How did Richie Kohler's "right way to live" differ from John Chatterton's? Did Kohler pass his own test?
- How would you have fared as a sailor on a German U-boat?

PART FOUR

LEADERSHIP

13

Last Voyage of the *La Conte*

The fishing was good; it was the catching that was bad.

A. K. Best

Something big is going down. US Coast Guard Lieutenant Steve Torpey can see it as he pulls up to park in front of the base in Sitka, Alaska. Lights are on across the base, people are running everywhere, and in the hangar two H-60 helicopters are receiving final checkups.

Torpey's two-year tour in Sitka is nearly over, and in recent days he's complained about missing out on every dramatic helicopter rescue they've launched. Now, as he rushes upstairs to the Operations Center, he wonders if he's finally going to have his chance.

The preflight briefing confirms it. A fishing boat has gone down sixty miles off Cape Fairweather during one of the most vicious storms in memory. Survivors are floating in the sea, buffeted by monster waves. One chopper attempted a rescue and failed. A second is on the scene. Torpey will be a pilot on the third chopper.

On his way out the door of the Operations Center, Torpey turns around. "Don't worry," he says. "We'll get them."

The day before—January 29, 1998—a man named Mark Morley made a fateful decision. Morley was skipper of the *La Conte*, an eighty-year-old fishing boat based in Sitka. The last run had been disappointing, and Morley was feeling pressure to make some money. He needed to pay his crew and the boat owner, and provide for his fiancée and her daughter. When he saw a window of clearing weather, he decided to make for the Fairweather Ground.

Mike DeCapua, one of the crew, was far from thrilled. The *La Conte* was a good boat in calm waters, but choppy waves on an open sea was something else. The *La Conte* had a nasty habit of taking on water in the engine-room bilge. It seemed like someone was always starting up the pump to push out seawater. Then there was the fact that the boat didn't have a life raft. But DeCapua liked Morley and understood his motivation. When Morley announced his intentions, DeCapua didn't protest.

The fishing was good that night off Fairweather—so good that Morley decided to stay longer than planned and lay out more skates of freshly baited gear.

By morning, a west wind was slamming twelve-foot swells against the *La Conte*. DeCapua was hooking frozen blocks of herring bait to a line when he glanced up at the sky. The sight gave him a chill. Seemingly at the end of the heavens, just above the sea, a menacing black line stretched across the horizon.

"Mark, do you see that black line?" DeCapua said. "That means we've got really heavy weather approaching. It's time to run back in. That's death coming!"

"No!" Morley yelled from the wheelhouse window. "We've just got a few more sets to make!"

"This is the Fairweather Ground," DeCapua fired back. "Gig and I have fished it all our lives. That black line is a

158

real bad sign, and it's coming this way. It's time to get out of here! Why don't we cut our losses? We can come back later and pick up our gear."

"No. We've got to get our gear up before we leave."

DeCapua said no more. By the time the last skate was reeled in, the swells had risen to twenty-five feet.

The storm grew worse. Morley finally aimed for shore, but rising swells and fifty-mile-an-hour winds combined with their catch of several thousand pounds held the *La Conte* in place. Then the wind and waves increased even more. The engine simply wasn't strong enough; they began to lose ground. Morley and his crew—deck boss Gig Mork, former Coast Guard supply officer Bob Doyle, Dave Hanlon, and DeCapua—were being swept out to sea.

At 6:30 that night, in darkness and with the storm raging, DeCapua and Doyle moved to the stern to check the engine room. DeCapua, in front, descended the steps and almost immediately plunged into icy water. The pump had stopped working. The engine room was flooding.

The crew rushed to form a bucket brigade, throwing water overboard as fast as possible. It was no use. They were sinking.

Morley issued a mayday. Doyle grabbed the Emergency Position Indicating Radio Beacon (EPIRB). Everyone scrambled into survival suits.

"We are going to stick together!" Morley shouted over eighty-mile-an-hour winds. "We're going to tie ourselves together with rope line and abandon this vessel together."

DeCapua had the only suit with five fingers. He began tying, leaving about nine feet of space between each man. Suddenly he clutched Doyle's arm.

"How about some buoys? We can tie them off to us. They'll keep us afloat."

"Good idea," Doyle said. He scrambled onto the roof of the pilothouse and began unknotting the buoy balls. The storm raged around him, throwing the *La Conte* up and down with ease.

Doyle felt a lump in his throat. He tried to swallow and couldn't. He tried desperately to hurry. *How are you supposed to take apart a rope wearing a three-fingered Gumby mitten?* he thought. *All right. Relax. Relax. I guess we should have headed in earlier. I guess it was nuts all right to be fishing with something this bad coming at you. I should have got that job in the auto supply store. Oh, sure. Order car parts for a living. Who drives in Alaska? I ought to live on the ocean. Why not? I'm going to die on it.*

There. I got it. Two buoy balls coming right down.

Doyle climbed down to the others, fighting to keep his feet. DeCapua tied one buoy to Hanlon. Doyle attached the other to himself.

The *La Conte* began to roll. Her crew moved to the high side of the port deck. Then the *La Conte* turned completely on her side. As she did, five men crawled atop the port side railing. Below them was a dark, roiling abyss.

It was time to leave.

"On the count of three, we all go in together!" Morley shouted. "One! Two!"

The *La Conte* began rolling.

"Now!"

They jumped. Suddenly they were in the black and icy Pacific Ocean, riding sixty-foot waves and fighting for their lives.

At the Sitka Coast Guard station, Torpey learns his flying partner is the base commander, Captain Ted Le Feuvre. There are no other pilots left. Torpey finds himself in the uncomfortable position of wondering about the captain's readiness to fly in extreme conditions. Le Feuvre is an experienced and accomplished pilot, but with his focus in recent months on his duties as commander, he's logged only a fraction of the flying time of the other base pilots.

Torpey and Le Feuvre approach the remaining H-60 in the hangar. Le Feuvre climbs up and begins strapping in.

"Captain," Torpey says, "how do you feel about that right seat there?"

Le Feuvre stops and turns to look at Torpey. His expression is calm.

"Steve, I understand exactly where you're coming from," he says. "I'd probably be doing the same thing if I were in your shoes."

Le Feuvre unbuckles, climbs out, and moves to the copilot seat on the left. Torpey is grateful for his captain's support. With lives at stake, this is no time for ego.

A few minutes after midnight, Le Feuvre keys his radio. "We're launching, boys. Hang on."

Their team is better prepared than the first two chopper teams. The five-man crew includes an extra flight mechanic, chemical "glow sticks" so the survivors will see the rescue basket in the dark, twenty-six flares that will burn for fifty minutes, and seven hundred pounds of extra fuel.

Less than an hour later, they are on-site, looking for the survivors and a blinking EPIRB beacon and battling the biggest waves they've ever seen.

There are only four survivors now. Dave Hanlon was already struggling with a leak in the hood of his survival suit. Then another monster wave sent them all underwater. When they surfaced and sounded off, Hanlon didn't answer. The rest realized Hanlon had somehow slipped from the rope loop. They searched and shouted, but there was no response.

He was gone.

Morley is also in a bad spot. The *La Conte*, as if taking revenge on its skipper, ripped a hole in the knee of his suit right after their desperate plunge from the dying ship. Morley's suit is steadily filling with thirty-eight-degree seawater.

"I'm not going to make it," Morley says. A moment later, he closes his eyes. He appears unconscious.

"Mark!" shouts Bob Doyle. "Mark, what's up?" Doyle slaps Morley's face. There's no reaction.

When each new wave crashes over them, Doyle holds a hand over Morley's mouth as long as possible, trying to prevent him from drowning. Then the wave forces them down and tears Morley away. When Doyle surfaces, he searches frantically for Morley. The pattern continues, Doyle growing more exhausted with each bombardment.

On the H-60, Torpey can't believe the size of the waves just below him. While flying in a hurricane in the Gulf of Mexico, he'd seen forty-foot waves and experienced seventy-mile-per-hour winds. But these waves are at least eighty feet, and the gusts are over a hundred miles an hour. It's taking all his concentration to keep the chopper level and in the vicinity of the survivors.

The crew deploys two rounds of flares, tiny lights that begin rising and falling on the surface below. Suddenly, a massive gust tilts the chopper's nose thirty degrees higher. In the next instant, the H-60 is thrown backward at an angle toward the sea.

Three crew members in the back of the helicopter yell over each other's voices: "Altitude! Up! Up! Up!"

Torpey and Le Feuvre nearly twist the collective out of the floor. They need lift power *now*!

Through the transparent bubble at his feet, Torpey watches the Pacific Ocean rise to claim another victim. The sea is forty feet away, perhaps less.

Well, Lord, I'm going to meet you, Le Feuvre prays. *But do I have to go out being cold and wet?*

Just when it seems they are going down, the H-60 recovers and begins to climb. They've been blown three thousand feet downwind of the survivors. It takes twenty minutes to fight their way back.

Both pilots know that trying to pluck exhausted survivors out of the sea in the midst of hurricane winds and rogue waves is pushing the limits of their abilities and their machine. They're well aware of the Coast Guard choppers that went down in recent years in Prince William Sound and off the coast of Oregon. In both cases, there were no survivors.

Le Feuvre has an inspiration. He proposes dividing pilot responsibilities—Le Feuvre will man the collective and focus on altitude while Torpey works the joystick and main controls. It's against the rule book and considered dangerous, but it's also a way to share the burden of flying.

"All right," Torpey says. "Why not?"

For the next hour, Torpey listens for the directions of flight engineer Fred Kalt as they try to drop a metal rescue basket near the survivors. The wind and waves make the job nearly impossible. Most often, the basket swings away wildly, sometimes dangerously close to the rear of the chopper. At other times, in total darkness, Torpey watches flares rise above the chopper. It means a giant wave is about to crest over them—it's time to gain altitude pronto, and the basket is yanked out of the sea.

Finally, seven and a half hours after the crew of the *La Conte* plunged into the sea, Kalt and Torpey score a hit. The basket lands ten yards from the four survivors. Torpey maneuvers the chopper to bring it even closer.

In the water, Doyle knows this is his one chance. He wraps his legs around Morley and pulls a knife from his survival suit.

"Bob, you take Mark!" Mork yells. "You're a better swimmer than I am. Take him to the basket!"

Perhaps sensing the moment, Morley suddenly revives. Doyle is astonished.

"We're going to do it, Mark!" Doyle shouts.

"You're darn right we're going to do it," Morley answers.

Doyle drags Morley down the face of a swell to the basket. He tries to push the skipper inside, but because of his exhaustion and the water weighing down Morley's suit, he can't do it.

Instead, Doyle climbs into the basket and, from his knees, grabs Morley's arms and pulls. Morley's arms and elbows are in over the lip of the basket when the ocean suddenly falls away. The basket, hooked to the H-60 by a 150-foot cable and pummeled by waves and wind, is swinging, spinning, and rising. Morley, out of strength, is dangling from the edge with only Doyle's lifesaving grip to keep him there.

"Don't drop me, Bob!" Morley says, his eyes locked on Doyle's. "Please don't drop me!"

From the chopper, Kalt can barely see the basket through the sleet, snow, and spray, but it appears someone's inside. It hoists closer and closer until it's even with the chopper's open door. But when he tries to slide it inside, something holds it up. Even with another crewman assisting, they can't haul the basket through the doorway.

Mike Fish, a Coast Guard swimmer, can't figure it out either. Then, through an opening between Kalt's right leg and the doorway, he sees why the basket won't come in. There's a man dangling from the far end. Every time they pull on the basket, the man's head is slammed against the fiberglass airframe of the chopper.

For an instant, Mike Fish stares into the eyes of Mark Morley. They reveal a man at the end of everything.

"Fred!" Fish shouts. "There's someone hanging on the basket!"

But it's too late. In the next instant, Morley is gone.

Fish reads the altimeter, measuring the distance to the water: 103 feet.

The basket is hauled in. Bob Doyle, now alone, is sobbing. "The skipper," he says. "The skipper just fell. I let him go! I let him go!"

Torpey maneuvers back until he can see a body floating arms out and facedown in the water. The body isn't moving.

"Sir, who do you want us to go for next?" Kalt asks.

Torpey is sure the skipper is either unconscious or dead. He has to choose. "Let's go for the two guys next to the EPIRB."

Twenty minutes later, Mork and DeCapua are climbing into the basket when a towering breaker slams into them. Mork hangs on and rides to the chopper, but DeCapua is washed away. A few minutes later, DeCapua is at last ready to give up and go to sleep when the basket suddenly drops in front of him. Somehow he finds the strength to swim and climb in. Soon he too is on board the H-60.

The rescuers aren't done. They lower the basket repeatedly, sometimes bumping it into Morley's body. They even try scooping him with it. But every attempt fails, and Morley never moves.

Le Feuvre has been watching the fuel gauge. They've already stayed too long to return to Sitka. Now they're minutes away from not having enough fuel to land anywhere.

"Hey, Steve," Le Feuvre says in a low voice, "it's time for us to go."

"Captain?"

"No, Steve. I said it's time to go."

Kalt's voice breaks in on the intercom. "No, wait, wait. I almost got him that time. We can do this. We can do this, sir!"

"No, Mr. Kalt." This time Le Feuvre's voice is harder.

"Captain," Torpey says again. "We can get this guy."

"No," Le Feuvre says. "It's time to go. *Now*."

Torpey reluctantly releases the controls to Le Feuvre. Through the bubble, Torpey watches the H-60 pass over the lifeless body of Mark Morley, which grows ever smaller in his vision as the chopper rises into the turbulent sky. Then the chopper is roaring into the madness of the storm.

Torpey flips off the floodlight and lets out a long, deep sigh.

Would You? Could You?

(Share your answers if you're reading in a group)

Every leader has to make tough calls. In the midst of a crisis, those decisions sometimes mean the difference between who lives and who dies. On that battered helicopter over the Fairweather Ground in 1998, Steve Torpey made the hard choice to focus on two for-sure breathing men before trying to rescue the skipper they'd lost. Ted Le Feuvre made the difficult decision to leave Morley behind and head home rather than put his team at further risk. Could Morley have been saved if they'd chosen differently? Maybe. Would a different approach have cost the lives of *everyone* on board? Very possibly. Living with those uncertainties is part of the duty of a leader.

Are you cut out to be this kind of leader? *Would you* have made the same choices as Torpey and Le Feuvre? *Could you* leave a man behind and live with the consequences?

- Anyone in the Coast Guard or military, or on a police force or fire department staff, knows they may be called to risk their lives for others. But how far should those in authority go to recover someone in need? Where would you draw the line?
- All three chopper commanders decided against putting a Coast Guard swimmer in the water off Cape Fairweather, fearing they might not get him back. Was it the right choice?
- Mark Morley failed to heed the warning of a crewman, while Ted Le Feuvre responded to Steve Torpey's question by giving up his pilot's seat. If you were in authority, how would you react? Would you be offended or appreciate the honest input?
- Le Feuvre's recommendation to divide the helicopter controls was radical and risky. If the mission had ended badly, he could have been blamed for the failure. When,

if ever, should a leader abandon protocol? Are you willing to go against convention even if it might cost you later?

- Le Feuvre could have ripped into his crew for knocking Morley off the basket. Instead, seeing how badly they felt, he encouraged them, saying, "You have delivered three people back to their families . . . you've given those children back their fathers. You cannot do any greater thing than that." Were those the right words? How does a leader know when to criticize and when to pat on the back?

- Bob Doyle was distraught after dropping Mark Morley (Morley's body was recovered the next day). Morley's fiancée was thankful to Doyle and the Coast Guard for trying so hard. If you were a member of Morley's family, would you blame Doyle and the Coast Guard or would you offer gratitude and forgiveness?

- Would you consider a career in the Coast Guard or in another field that requires dangerous rescues? Why or why not?

Reporting In

Someday, somewhere, you will be called upon to make life-altering decisions in an instant. Pray now for the Lord's guidance and wisdom for that moment.

Hitting the Trail

(This is just for you)

When Solomon was king of Israel, God appeared to him and directed him to ask for anything. Solomon answered, "Give me wisdom and knowledge, that I may lead this people" (2 Chron. 1:10). And so the Lord did, along with "wealth, riches and honor" (v. 12). If wisdom and knowledge were essential to one of the Bible's great kings, maybe now is a good time to see where they fit in *your* life as a leader.

- Write down the ways that you are a leader today, whether you're a class officer, captain of a team, or simply someone whom friends or siblings occasionally look up to. Are you growing in these areas by adding to your "wisdom and knowledge"? If not, what could you be doing to grow?

  _____

  _____

  _____

  _____

- Look to the future and write down leadership roles that you might like to be in someday. You might be a company manager, a military officer, a husband or wife, a father or mother, or a church or community volunteer. How can you add wisdom now that will help you then? What knowledge can you begin to acquire today that will prepare you?

  _____

  _____

  _____

- Who in your life do you see as a wise leader? Why? Who lacks wisdom as a leader? Who are knowledgeable and unknowledgeable leaders in your eyes? How would you be different?

  _____

  _____

  _____

New Territory

(For those who want to explore further)

Read Todd Lewin's *The Last Run* or Spike Walker's *Coming Back Alive*, which both tell of the Coast Guard's dramatic rescue attempts of the crew of the *La Conte* in 1998.

- Who were the most and least impressive leaders during this incident? Why?
- What lessons could you draw from the experiences of these men?

14

Boy Wonder

You have to do your own growing no
matter how tall your grandfather was.

Abraham Lincoln

D ad. Wake up. Wake up."
Never in his eleven-plus years had Norman Ollestad
Jr. needed his father more than this moment. Minutes before, the four passengers of the chartered Cessna—
Norman Ollestad Sr.; his girlfriend, Sandra Cressman; pilot
Rob Arnold; and Norman Jr.—were flying through a storm
in California's San Gabriel Mountains. They couldn't see
anything through the clouds. Then, suddenly, the Cessna was
pinging off trees and breaking into pieces.

Norman had come to surrounded by fog and snow, still
strapped into his seat. A tree stretched across the instrument
panel in front of him. The pilot was dead. Sandra was sobbing from somewhere above him. And his father was slumped
against the back of Norman's seat.

"What are we going to do, Norman?" thirty-year-old Sandra had wailed.

Norman's dad would know what to do. He was a man of action—an adventurer and former FBI agent who had repeatedly pushed his young son to success in the surf and on the slopes, and who had once managed to strand the two of them in a Mexican jungle without food or money. Norman sometimes complained about this thrill-seeking existence. He longed for a normal life. But they were the dynamic duo, his dad a superhero and Norman his father's "Boy Wonder."

Now it's February 19, 1979, they're crashed on top of a mountain in the middle of a blizzard, and Norm Sr. isn't acting like a hero. He isn't doing or saying anything. Norman puts his hand on his dad's back and can't tell whether he's even breathing.

"Daddy," he whispers. But there's no answer. He kisses his father and holds him for a long time.

Finally, an instinct deep inside Norman begins to surface. His mind isn't ready to let go, to admit that he's on his own, to face this ever-deepening nightmare. But another part of him is already moving toward survival. It knows a ski racing sweater and Vans sneakers won't protect him long. It knows he is cold and getting colder.

He turns away from his father then and crouches on all fours like an animal. He studies his surroundings, blocking out all other thoughts, and sees that there may be shelter under a nearby wing. He tries to lift his dad, but he doesn't have the strength. He gives up and crawls to Sandra.

Norman takes Sandra's hand and releases her seat belt. "Let's go," he says, pulling.

"What are you doing?" she says.

"Move with me. We're crossing to the wing. We can get under it."

Ten minutes later, Norman and Sandra are sitting under the wing, huddled together for warmth. Soon Norman drifts into a restless sleep.

He's awakened by a rhythmic thumping sound.

"What's going to happen to us, Norman?" Sandra says. She has a bloody gash on her forehead near the part line of her brown hair. Her right shoulder slants at a strange angle. It's probably dislocated.

The thumping gets louder.

Norman scrambles out from under the wing. "I hear a helicopter," he says.

Through the shifting fog, Norman makes out the belly of a chopper directly above them. He waves his arms over his head.

"Hey! Right here! Hey!"

The helicopter turns and tips so Norman can actually see a helmeted figure inside. Norman motions toward the crash site and begins moving in that direction. But then the helicopter turns and slowly drifts away. They didn't see him.

Norman shifts his gaze from the sky to his dad, now only fifteen feet away. "Can you believe that?" he says aloud.

He looks closer. His father hasn't moved. He's covered with snow.

Norman closes his eyes. He can't think about that.

If no one can find them at the top of this mountain, they're going to have to get down on their own. Norman studies the snow-covered gullies, ravines, and rocks that make up the steep slope, imagining a possible path. As his eyes trace an escape, he's amazed at what he sees in the distance. Perhaps two miles away, beyond a flat area that must be a meadow, is a rooftop.

The storm returns and fog sweeps away any sign of the roof. But Norman is sure he saw it.

"Are they coming back?" Sandra asks.

"I don't know. I saw a cabin."

"They'll come back for us."

Norman sits down and again huddles with Sandra. He doesn't know what to do.

Norman is swimming, but he can't break through the surface to the air above. Finally he allows himself to drift into the depths. At the bottom he feels safe and warm. It's so comfortable here.

No, his mind tells him. *Get up.*

Slowly, reluctantly, Norman stretches his body and opens his eyes.

Snow. The crash. His dad. Sandra.

"Get up!" he yells.

He shakes Sandra. "Get up! You can't sleep."

"Norman?" says an exhausted voice.

"Get up."

"I'm tired, Norman. Very tired."

"I know, but you can't sleep. My dad said when you freeze to death you feel warm and then you fall asleep and never wake up."

Sandra looks at him. "Big Norm is dead," she says.

Norman blocks out the words.

"We have to go now," he says.

"They're coming."

"They're not coming."

It's afternoon now. They need to get to that rooftop before dark. The only way down the mountain is to descend near the edge of a nearly vertical funnel that's slick with ice. It's snowing hard, making it difficult to see where the best and worst patches are. Sandra, Norman knows, wouldn't be much of a climber even on her best day.

But it is so cold. They have to find shelter.

"Sandra, we have to go," he says.

"No."

"I'm going."

"You can't leave me here."

"Then come on."

With frozen and stiff hands, Norman snaps two branches off a tree, breaks off the twigs, and hands one branch to Sandra. He shows her how to plunge the branch into the ice for traction and balance.

"I'll go below you," he says. "Use me to step on. Stay right above me so I can stop you from sliding. Okay?"

"Your face is cut open."

Norman fingers his face and finds frozen blood on his chin and cheek. "It's not bleeding," he says.

"Am I okay?"

"You're fine. Let's go."

Norman slowly descends, using the stick in one hand to test traction below and raising the other hand to hold one of Sandra's white leather boots. He tells her to inch down. Sandra comes down fast. The impact kicks out Norman's stick and they both begin to skid.

Norman jams his feet and hands into the snow to slow them down while pinning Sandra's boots to his shoulder with his head. They slide to a stop.

"You have to use the stick to ease down!" he says. "Don't lift it all the way up. Okay?"

"It's hard. I feel funny, Norman. Is there something wrong with my head?"

"No. Just hang in there. We're almost down."

Norman knows they're nowhere near the bottom.

They continue to descend until Norman realizes that Sandra is moving away from him and closer to the funnel. Her stick barely touches the slope.

"Get the stick down! Turn your hand down!"

It's too late. Sandra starts sliding toward the funnel. Norman pushes off, sideways and down, and again catches her boots on his shoulder. Once again, he's able to brake with his hands and feet in the snow.

After he catches his breath, he says, "You have to slide *straight* down, Sandra. Understand?"

"My arm is getting tired, Norman." Her voice wavers.

He glances up and sees they've descended only thirty feet since the last slip. At this rate, they'll still be on the slope when darkness falls. They won't have a chance.

"We gotta hustle," he says.

Norman saves Sandra twice more—one a short fall, the other longer. Now it's late afternoon, they are thousands of feet from the bottom, and they have maybe two hours of light left.

At least they are making progress. If only he weren't so exhausted.

It occurs to Norman that he can't feel Sandra's boot on his shoulder. He looks up. She's three or four feet above him.

"Sandra. Get the stick down. Push to your left."

She doesn't say anything. She pulls up her knees so that she's crouching on the slope. To stretch? To stand up? He doesn't know.

"No!" he yells. "Stay down!"

She doesn't. Instead, she falls headfirst. It all happens too fast.

Norman stabs the stick into the slope with his left hand. With his right hand, he lunges for Sandra. But her body shifts. His aim is off.

For an instant, he feels her fingers on his right arm, at the bicep. Then she's crashing over him. Then—last chance—he has his fingers on one boot.

"Norman!" she screams.

And then Sandra is gone.

Norman has lost his footing and is on his way to join her. His left hand closes around a small tree protruding from the slope. He stops sliding.

Through the fog, he hears his name again. It echoes and dies out.

Shock. Guilt. Shame. Loneliness. Fear. The feelings bounce around in Norman's mind like the echoes of Sandra's last shout.

But there is still the mountain, the treacherous ice, and the meadow and rooftop below. He has to focus. He has to keep moving, to descend before it gets dark.

He tries to hurry. His foot slips. Suddenly he's sliding on his stomach, feetfirst, fast. He flips over, trying to jam his heels into the ice. He rolls, hoping to find soft snow.

His knee catches on a rise in the slope. Suddenly he's airborne. Then he's back on the slope, still sliding, headfirst now.

He spins. He's starting to lose consciousness. Then he feels snow beneath him. Norman presses every available body part against the slope. Gradually, his speed slows until he finally brakes to a stop.

Dizzy, dazed, gulping air, he sits up.

I can't. I can't do this anymore.

His mind wants to rest, to sleep. But something inside says no. He can almost hear his dad's voice: "Go for it, Boy Wonder. You can do it."

It's less steep here. Norman finds a tree and breaks off two branches. He sits on his rear and begins an intentional slide. He uses his feet and the branches to maneuver. Soon he's zooming down the mountain again, this time controlling the descent.

He comes to a small cliff face. There's something blocking his route.

Sandra.

She's on her back, hair splayed out, skin purple, eyes open and staring at the sky.

Norman kneels beside her, shakes her.

"Are you there? Sandra. Sandra. Your eyes are open. You just slipped. You'll be all right. Let's go!"

Norman waits there on his knees. He's so tired of the struggle, of death, of everything. Time seems to stop.

Then, somewhere deep inside, the thing that won't let him rest returns. It erupts in a growl and forces him to his feet. He's moving again.

He finds a group of spruce trees and breaks off several branches. He lays these over Sandra's body. Maybe they will keep her warm.

"I have to go," he says.

More sliding, more falling, more down climbing. And suddenly the meadow is in sight, but it's protected by a moat of buckthorn topped with snow. Norman steps onto it and immediately plunges in up to his neck. He feels trapped until he figures out he can "swim" through the tangled vines. A few minutes later he reaches a hedge and uses it to pull himself across the buckthorn.

At last, at dusk, he reaches the meadow. He steps into the soft snow and walks along the meadow's edge, searching for a path.

He sees something in the snow and kneels. It's a boot print.

"Hello!" a voice calls out. "Anybody there?"

The sound echoes. Norman can't tell where it's coming from. He isn't sure it's real, but he answers anyway.

"Help! Help me!"

"Keep yelling! I'll follow your voice!"

Norman runs in the direction of the second shout. He stumbles onto a dirt road. From around a bend appears a brown dog, followed by a teenage boy in a jacket.

"Are you from the crash?" the boy asks.

"Yes."

"Is there anybody else up there?"

"Yes. My dad and his girlfriend, Sandra. The pilot's dead."

"What about your dad?"

The words are on Norman's lips before he stops to think.

"Dead or just knocked out. I shook him but he didn't wake up."

Saying it now, and watching the boy's face, suddenly makes it real. Norman knows his father is gone. He also realizes that he wouldn't be standing here, alive, if his father hadn't pushed him so hard all those years.

178

"Should I carry you?" the teenager asks.

"No, I'm fine," Norman says.

The teen picks him up anyway. Norman doesn't protest. Maybe, for just a few minutes, it will be okay to be an eleven-year-old boy again.

Would You? Could You?

(Share your answers if you're reading in a group)

Norman Ollestad had a father whom parents today might call both devoted and reckless. Norm Sr. was a man with a hunger for extremes who shared his zeal with his son. He took young Norman surfing in waves that broke over his head. He led Norman on ski runs across restricted avalanche fields. He had Norman steer the car while he slept. It left Norman wishing for the normal life of his friends, "riding bikes together after school, playing ball in a cul-de-sac." Yet the frightening experiences that made up his childhood were the same ones that saved his life after the plane crash on Ontario Peak in 1979. At the moment of crisis, it was eleven-year-old Norman who took charge and ultimately survived.

Today, though Norman's approach with his own preteen son is more measured, he sees the value of what he learned. "I definitely have the same instinct my father had, which is why I want to share these passions with my son," Norman says. "I think it's important to expose him to surfing, skiing, hockey, whatever it is. Because I know that down the line in his life, he will find beauty and pleasure when he needs it. And he'll always be able to go to these things, no matter what's going on in his life."

Beauty. Pleasure. An ability to adapt and survive in the most extreme environments. These are some of the benefits of outdoor adventure and pushing to the limit. Are they part of your life? *Should* they be?

- *Could you*, at the age of eleven, have kept from freaking out after the shock of a plane crash and the death of

179

your father? *Would you* have had the courage and skills needed to get down the mountain and survive?

- Norman says of growing up with his dad, "I was scared a lot of the time. That's the whole point. He showed me that being afraid is okay. You can either dance with it or you can run from it. In life it's better to dance, because even if you live a sheltered life, it's going to find you." Do you agree with this? Why or why not?

- What exactly are the beauty and pleasure that Norman talks about above? Is it something physical? Emotional? Spiritual? Do you experience it in your life? When?

- Norman insisted that Sandra join him in attempting to climb down the mountain. Given her skills and condition, was it the right decision? What would you have done?

- Almost from the beginning of the crisis, Sandra looked to Norman for inspiration and as the decision-maker on their small team. Was that inappropriate or unfair? If you had been in Sandra's position, what would you have done?

- How did your younger years compare to Norman's? Do we as a society underestimate or expect too little of our kids and teens? Explain.

Reporting In

Moses was a reluctant leader (see Exodus 3 and 4:1–17). Pray for trust and boldness so that you will be ready when the Lord calls on you to lead his people.

Hitting the Trail

(This is just for you)

In an interview, Norman Ollestad said, "The times I feel closest to [my father] actually is when I'm lost in the trees, skiing powder alone. I'll think of him. He's the one who showed me how to sniff that stuff out and gave me the passion for it."

Isn't that true of most of us? When we're lost and alone, we are most drawn to those who loved or still love us, to those who shaped our lives. It may be family or friends. It may also be our Father in heaven.

- Whom do you turn to when you are feeling lost or alone? Parents? Siblings? Friends? Jesus? Write down specific ways that they give you strength, support, and encouragement during the hard times.

  _____

  _____

  _____

- Bernard Martin has written, "To most people loneliness is a doom. Yet loneliness is the very thing which God has chosen to be one of the schools of training for His very own. It is the fire that sheds the dross and reveals the gold." Do you agree with this statement? Write down what it means to you.

  _____

  _____

  _____

- When have you been afraid and overcome your fear to develop a passion for something? Write down the process that allowed that to happen. What are you afraid of today? How could you overcome your fear?

  _____

  _____

  _____

New Territory

(For those who want to explore further)
Read Norman Ollestad's *Crazy for the Storm* and Nando Parrado's *Miracle in the Andes*.

- How did Norman's leadership challenge differ from the one faced by survivors of the plane crash in the Andes? How was it similar?
- The Andes survivors were older and had each other for support. Could they, at age eleven, have survived Norman's predicament? Why or why not?

15

Nightmare in Mogadishu

Teach me your way, O LORD;
lead me in a straight path because of my oppressors.

Psalm 27:11

Three military Humvees filled with US Army Rangers move at a steady pace through the narrow, unpaved streets of downtown Mogadishu, Somalia. The sounds of gunfire and explosions are everywhere. It seems as if the entire city is unloading its fury against the small convoy.

Ranger Sergeant Jeff Struecker, sitting in the right front seat, commands the lead vehicle. The twenty-four-year-old from Fort Dodge, Iowa, has already seen combat in Panama and the Persian Gulf, but he's never faced a scene like this. Bullets fill the air, many pinging off the metal exterior of the Humvees.

Private First Class Brad Paulson, from the Midwest, mans the .50-caliber machine gun at the top of the lead Humvee. He's swinging it back and forth, trying to return fire everywhere. "Paulson, just take the left side!" Struecker shouts.

"Pilla, you cover the right!" Sergeant Dominick Pilla is a large kid from New Jersey, known in the Ranger squadron for practical jokes and playing the lead in humorous skits. He's behind a metal bomb protection plate, shooting an M-60 machine gun out a side window.

The October 3, 1993, mission had started well. Task Force Rangers had been in Mogadishu for nearly two months as part of a United Nations effort to capture a warlord named Mohamed Farrah Aidid. The country was in chaos, ripped apart by competing factions. Aidid, who controlled the drug trade and food supplies, was the most powerful of the warlords.

In the past few weeks, the Ranger force had conducted six raids into the city, each time capturing one of Aidid's important associates. This time, an informant identified two targets meeting in the same location. It was a great opportunity. The drawback? It was downtown, a block north of the Olympic Hotel—right in the middle of Aidid's territory.

That afternoon eight Black Hawk helicopters and other gunships swooped in, dropping Delta Force operators (D-boys) and Rangers into the city. Struecker, meanwhile, had led a convoy of Humvees into the city. Once the D-boys secured the targets, the convoy's task was to transport the prisoners three miles back to the Ranger base. The whole operation involved 160 soldiers and was expected to take thirty minutes.

Everything seemed to go smoothly at the target house. The bad guys had been rounded up and were nearly ready for transport. Then Struecker got the word: the Rangers had a casualty. Private First Class Todd Blackburn, fresh out of a Florida high school and new to Mogadishu, had missed the rope coming out of a Black Hawk. He'd fallen seventy feet and was severely injured and unconscious. Struecker was ordered to load Blackburn onto a backboard and into a cargo Humvee, then take two more Humvees and return to base.

Struecker instructed Private First Class Jeremy Kerr, his driver, to move at a deliberate pace. "We need to take it slow, so we don't break Blackburn's neck," he said. "Dodge every pothole you can." But the enemy fire was intense. At some points they had to blast through makeshift barricades.

Now they have covered five blocks and are making the final turn onto a boulevard that will lead them out of the slums and back "home." As they turn, Pilla spots a gunman pointing an AK-47 at him. Pilla quickly aims. Both men fire at virtually the same moment.

Struecker hears Specialist Tim Moynihan screaming, "Pilla's hit! He's shot in the head!"

Struecker glances back. Pilla is slumped into Moynihan's lap. Blood is everywhere.

"What do we do? Dom's killed!" Moynihan yells. Kerr and Paulson begin talking excitedly as well.

Struecker senses the situation getting out of control. For a moment, he starts to panic himself. A good soldier and friend, a man he is responsible for, is dead. He swallows. But then he realizes he needs to put all that out of his mind. *Take charge, Jeff,* he thinks.

"Moynihan," he says. "Stop what you're doing. Take your weapon and face right; pick up Dominick's sector of fire. Kerr, step on it! Fly down this road as fast as you can!" It was time to forget worrying about a bumpy ride making Blackburn's injury worse. They needed to concentrate on getting out of there.

A few minutes later, the three Humvees roar through the gate to the Ranger base. A medical team approaches and begins pulling Pilla's body out of the back of the vehicle.

"Just leave him alone," Struecker says. "He's gone. Go to the other vehicle. Blackburn's over there."

Struecker can't believe what just happened. Pilla is the first Ranger casualty in Mogadishu. The sergeant walks away from the Humvee, takes off his helmet, and hurls it against a stack of sandbags. *God, like, so what's the deal here? How come this all fell apart on me?*

He turns and realizes the remainder of his squad is staring at him. They've never seen him lose control before.

A lieutenant approaches. His face is pale. Slowly, he says, "Another Black Hawk has gone down. You need to get your squad ready to go back in. We need to get to the crash site."

"What do you mean, *another*?" Struecker learns that Aidid's militia has taken down two helicopters in the city with RPGs (rocket propelled grenades). No one knows how many Rangers survived the crashes, and Aidid's men are closing in quickly.

Oh no, Struecker thinks. They've already lost one man; the rest of his team barely escaped. Now they're being ordered to revisit a nightmare. Yet Struecker knows that now more than ever, he can't let his men see his concern.

"Sergeant Mitchell!" he says. "Get your vehicle down to the supply point and get more ammo! Get some for us too, while you're at it. And don't forget to fuel up.

"Moynihan! Thomas! Go get some water, and make sure there's nothing in the vehicles that's not absolutely mission-essential! Get some night vision goggles too. This might take a while." The men hesitate for a moment, then move into action.

A Delta Force operator walks over. "Sergeant, you don't want to take your men back out in all that blood. You need to clean up your vehicle first."

Struecker glances at the Humvee and the evidence of Pilla's grisly death. He realizes the operator is right—his men are psyched out enough. "Roger that," he says.

He turns to Kerr and Paulson, both probably nineteen years old. He can see in their eyes that they're overwhelmed. How can he order them to take on this job?

"Men," Struecker says, "I could use some help cleaning up this vehicle—but I'm not going to make you do it. If you want to volunteer, okay. But if you'd rather not, I understand. Just go help load up more fuel and ammo instead."

Both privates stay with Struecker as he drives the Humvee to a water tanker. Using a sponge, a yellow brush, buckets of water, and their bare hands, the men go to work. Pilla's ammo can is still in the Humvee, filled with blood and unused bullets. *Man, we're gonna need this,* Struecker thinks. He pulls out the ammo and dumps it in a bucket of clean water.

The radio is broadcasting news from the fight in Mogadishu. Most of it isn't good. By the sound of the reports, Struecker estimates there may be up to ten thousand Somalis battling the small Ranger force. He finally tells Kerr to turn the radio off.

I'm going to die tonight, Struecker thinks. *And what's just as bad, I'm going to get every one of my men killed. I just know it. There's no way we can survive another run back into that city. Tomorrow this squad is going to have ten dead Rangers instead of just one.*

Struecker's thoughts shift to his pregnant wife, Dawn, back at the Ranger base at Fort Benning, Georgia. *My child is never going to know his daddy. This is it, tonight. How is she going to manage having a baby and raising it all by herself?*

He begins to pray silently. *God, I'm in deep trouble, as you can see. I need help. I'm not saying you should get me out of this. I just need your help.*

His mind returns to the Rangers in his charge. *God, please don't let me do anything stupid that puts the rest of my men into a slaughter tonight. If any of them get killed, I sure don't want it to be my fault.* Struecker doesn't hear a response to his prayer, at least not in words. Yet he's pleased to discover a renewed sense of peace.

He inspects the cleaned-out Humvee. "Men, we're good. Let's load up and get ready to move."

Specialist Brad Thomas got married a few months ago. He'd been on the beach with Pilla earlier in the day. When the Humvees pulled into the base with Pilla's splattered remains, Thomas was crying. Now he approaches Struecker.

"Sergeant, you know I *really* don't want to go back out," he says.

Struecker isn't surprised by Thomas's statement. There will be serious consequences for any Ranger who asks out of a mission. But Thomas is expressing what everyone is thinking.

Struecker feels eyes on him, watching to see how he'll react. He could end the specialist's career right here. He tries a different approach.

"Listen," he says in a low voice. "I understand how you feel. I'm married too. Don't think of yourself as a coward. I know you're scared. I've never been in a situation quite like this either. But we've got to go. It's our job. The difference between being a coward and being a hero is not whether you're scared or not. It's what you do while you're scared."

Thomas walks away, and Struecker mounts his Humvee. A minute later, Struecker glances into his rearview mirror. He sees Thomas climbing aboard one of the other Humvees. The convoy is ready to go.

Struecker and his men lead the way back into the city, where they survive withering fire and an RPG that skips across the hood of their Humvee. They encounter the remains of the original convoy, which had been searching for the first downed Black Hawk and is now shot to pieces. The mission changes for Struecker and his convoy; they're ordered to transport the wounded from the original convoy back to base.

At 11:30 that night, Struecker's Humvee leads a convoy into the city for the third time. Rangers from the downed Black Hawks and early rescue attempts are still in Mogadishu. Some are dead, but the Ranger motto is "leave no man behind"—dead or alive. Struecker's Humvee is the first vehicle in and, after one of the longest nights anyone can remember, the very last to leave.

On the way out, while still taking fire from the enemy, Paulson yells from his position atop the Humvee, "Sergeant! We've got bodies chasing after us from down the street."

"Open fire," Struecker says.

"Sergeant, I think these are our guys!"

Struecker turns to look. He can't believe it. About a dozen Rangers are running in their direction. Somehow they hadn't been picked up. He can see the terror in their eyes.

The rest of the convoy moves on, but Struecker's Humvee and another turn back. In the midst of some of the heaviest fire

188

of the mission, they quickly round up the remaining Rangers and finally, mercifully, return to base. Behind them, the streets are virtually covered by thousands of empty brass shell casings. They glisten in the morning sunlight.

Would You? Could You?

(Share your answers if you're reading in a group)

There's nothing that twists your gut quite like the knowledge that you're going into a hairy situation with an excellent chance of not coming back out. The members of the United Nations force in Somalia in October 1993 faced exactly that feeling. Eighteen US soldiers died and another seventy-three were injured during the battle in Mogadishu. In Sergeant Jeff Struecker's squad, Brad Paulson and another gunner were wounded. Dominick Pilla was the lone death. Struecker was awarded a Bronze Star for Valor for his service.

The men in Struecker's squad came to know that gut-twisting particularly well. After the first raid, they knew what they were up against in downtown Mogadishu. It was far more intense than anything they'd encountered before. When the order came to go back—and later, to go back again—they had to confront their fear and mortality. Struecker had an additional burden. He not only had to face down his own frustration and fear but also inspire the remaining eight Rangers in his squad, as well as others recruited to join the new convoys.

Leadership styles are as varied as the men and women who lead. Some rule with an iron fist. Some employ encouragement. Others lead by example. Many attempt a combination of these and other techniques. Whatever the method, we all know the value of strong leadership, especially during times of crisis. How do *you* respond to a crisis? If you were Jeff Struecker in October 1993, how would you have fared as the bullets blazed during the battle in Mogadishu?

- Have you ever had to lead others in a life-or-death situation? How did you handle it? Does having that extra

189

responsibility make it harder or easier to function during a crisis?

- On two occasions during the Mogadishu conflict—when Pilla's blood had to be cleaned up and when Thomas confronted him—Sergeant Struecker gave his men a choice instead of an order. Was it the right strategy? How could it have backfired?

- After Jesus Christ washed the feet of his disciples, he said, "I have set you an example that you should do as I have done for you. I tell you the truth, no servant is greater than his master, nor is a messenger greater than the one who sent him" (John 13:15–16). How did Struecker demonstrate this kind of servant leadership when he joined his men in cleaning the Humvee? What did it say to his men? Was it worth the time he could have spent preparing for the upcoming mission?

- As a Ranger, Struecker was trained to not show fear in front of his men. Today, however, he advocates an approach that combines toughness, control, and honesty: "I've learned that subordinates relate much better to me when I'm not trying to be so stoic. They appreciate knowing that I have to deal with fear just as they do." Do you agree with that approach? Why or why not? How does it compare to how you lead friends, fellow students, or teammates?

- As a born-again Christian (and now a US Army chaplain), Jeff Struecker has endured the taunts and behind-the-back comments of fellow soldiers who don't understand his faith. How does being a Christian affect one's ability to lead non-Christians? What are the obstacles? What are the advantages?

Reporting In

When was the last time you provided an example of servant leadership? If you can't remember, maybe it's time to ask the

Lord to send you an opportunity. While you're at it, ask him how you're doing as a leader and ambassador for him.

Hitting the Trail

(This is just for you)

Leadership is a tricky business. Jeff Struecker has advocated toughness, control, and honesty—yet in Mogadishu, he at times demonstrated compassion (to Brad Thomas) and frustration (when he threw his helmet), and he kept his fears to himself. Finding the right approach for each situation may be the greatest leadership challenge of all.

- Who are the leaders in your life who most inspire you? Why do you admire and respect them? Write down their names and what it is about them and their approach that moves you. Is Christ on your list? Why or why not?

  _____

  _____

  _____

  _____

- Think about the people you are called on to lead. What leadership style do they respond to best? Write down your answers. How are you at delivering that style? Write that down too.

  _____

  _____

  _____

- Here's the big one—what can you do in the next week to improve your leadership technique? Do you need to

191

work on being tougher, more in control, or more open and honest? Record your thoughts here.

_____

_____

_____

New Territory

(For those who want to explore further)

Read Mark Bowden's bestseller *Black Hawk Down* or Jeff Struecker's *The Road to Unafraid*. If you don't mind some grisly scenes, watch the Columbia Pictures movie *Black Hawk Down*.

- There were many tests of leadership throughout the conflict in Somalia in 1993. Who do you feel passed the test? Who failed? If some of the decisions had changed, how might things have turned out differently?
- Is there a conflict between the life of a soldier and the calling of a Christian? Is there such a thing as a "just" war? Was the United Nations intervention in Somalia such a war? What do you base your answers on?

16

The Expedition

He who has compassion on them will guide
them and lead them beside springs of water.

Isaiah 49:10

Standing on an Antarctic ice floe, his breath appearing
in small clouds of white, Ernest Shackleton watches his
men feed their sled dogs. A movement in the distance
catches his eye.

It is the *Endurance*—and she is sinking. The stout Norwegian schooner has carried Shackleton and his twenty-seven
crew members thirteen thousand miles to this forlorn spot
in the Weddell Sea. They are only one day's sail from their
intended destination, Antarctica's Vashel Bay, from which
Shackleton had hoped to launch the first overland expedition
across the continent.

But five months after departing England in the summer
of 1914, the *Endurance* was thwarted by an unusually severe
winter and trapped in the polar ice. No amount of effort
could free her. For the past ten months, Shackleton and his

mates have endured in the subzero conditions as they waited for their frozen prison to release them.

The wait was in vain. A few weeks earlier, the vise grip around the *Endurance* tightened; she was being crushed by ice. The men were forced to abandon ship. Now their lone symbol of civilization is disappearing—and with it the faint hope of restoring their former home.

"She's going, boys!" Shackleton shouts. He dashes up a lookout tower. The crew scrambles out of tents pitched on the frozen wasteland and watches silently. Across the ice pack, the stern of *Endurance* rises twenty feet into the air, her propeller and rudder clearly visible. Then, slowly, she is devoured by the sea. Less than ten minutes after Shackleton's shout, there is no trace of the schooner. Ice closes up the black hole of open water that marked her grave.

The sight is heartbreaking for all. Shackleton is so devastated that later, in his journal, he notes that "I cannot write about it." In front of his charges, however, Shackleton shows no sign of disappointment or loss. "Ship and stores have gone," he tells them, "so now we'll go home."

It is a typical Shackleton moment. The expedition leader is adapting to the circumstances, giving his men what they need most—confident direction delivered in a calm voice. It is not the first such moment on this journey, nor will it be the last.

From the beginning of the expedition, Shackleton has worked to mold his men into a cohesive unit. He broke down typical divisions between officers and crew, sailors and scientists, by requiring everyone to pitch in on ship's work. Seamen would take hydrographic readings. Doctors and scientists would do their share of chores, night watches, and turns at the helm. Shackleton also rotated work assignments to encourage multiple friendships and prevent cliques. The trust and camaraderie they built up soon served them well.

When the *Endurance* became trapped, Shackleton fought against anxiety, boredom, and dissension by promoting games

194

on the ice floes: soccer, hockey, and dog races. He also continued to celebrate birthdays, holidays, and other special events. Meteorologist Leonard Hussey entertained with his banjo. Despite adversity, the men were content, even happy. They were living proof of one of Shackleton's core beliefs: "Adventure is the soul of existence because it [brings] out true harmony among men."

Then came the day the ice wrapped itself tighter around the *Endurance*, warping her sides and wringing animal-like screams from her beams. A band of emperor penguins watched the tortured ship and uttered a series of mournful cries unknown to all on board. "Do you hear that?" one crew member said. "We'll none of us get back to our homes again."

The men lowered their three lifeboats, gathered what supplies they could, and congregated on the sturdiest-looking ice floe. Shackleton could see the discouragement in their faces. He addressed the group, calmly explaining his plans and what they were up against. He rallied them with what one expedition member described as a "simple, moving, optimistic, and highly effective" speech.

After the sinking of the *Endurance*, the men at least know what they are up against. It falls to them to pull themselves out of their predicament.

The next five-and-a-half months are a sentence of useless attempts to cross the dangerous, uneven ice floes on foot, followed by endless waiting. As they wait, the ice pack gradually drifts northwest.

Finally, as the Antarctic summer moves into fall, the warmed-up ice begins to break apart. The expedition's ice floe, once a mile in diameter, is now less than two hundred yards across. The men ready the three lifeboats and hope for a channel of open water. There is no time to lose; the current is taking them away from the series of small islands along Antarctica's northwest tip and toward the open sea.

On the evening of April 8, 1916, the ice floe splits. Two boats are hurried across the crack so the group can stay together. The next morning, the floe splits again as other floes grind against it. The men watch as ice and water jockey for position. At 12:40 in the afternoon, Shackleton quietly gives the order: "Launch the boats." There is no turning back. If the ice closes again, the lifeboats will be crushed, along with any hope of survival.

In the first thirty minutes, the rowers in the three small boats make gradual progress; the ice seems to loosen further. Many are admiring a flat-top iceberg close by when a low roar attracts all eyes to starboard. Bearing down on them is a lavalike flow of tumbling ice, at least two feet high and wide as a river. It's a riptide, and it can easily sink them all.

Shackleton swings his boat around and shouts for the others to do the same. It's a race for survival. The oarsmen dig in, four in each boat, pulling with all their strength. They are facing astern, staring straight at their enemy. Twice the *Dudley Docker*, the most cumbersome boat to row, is nearly overtaken. After fifteen minutes, when the oarsmen have nearly nothing left, the riptide loses some of its fury. Five minutes later, it flattens out. Fresh rowers take over, and the boats resume their original course.

It is the beginning of seven days of misery. On the first night, the men are able to pitch tents on a floe. Shackleton takes the first watch, sleeps for an hour, then gets up again to survey the floe. He seems inexhaustible, forever watching and planning on behalf of his party.

His vigilance saves the life of crewman Ernie Holness. In the darkness, a large swell strikes the floe. "Crack!" someone yells. The split widens underneath a tent. Holness, in his sleeping bag, falls into icy water. Shackleton rushes forward, throws himself onto the edge of the ice, grabs the bag, and heaves Holness out of the water. A moment later, another swell cements the crack in the floe back together.

Later, in the boats, Captain Frank Worsley uses a sextant to determine the expedition's position. On the third day, despite rowing west, they are twenty-two miles east of their former camp on the ice—they're being swept toward open ocean. That night, when the moon peeks through the clouds, Shackleton takes stock of his men. They are wet, cold, hungry, thirsty, and exhausted from rowing and lack of sleep. Lips are cracked, eyes red, faces crusted with salt. Some are suffering the first signs of frostbite.

"In the momentary light, I could see their ghostly faces," Shackleton later wrote in his journal. "I doubted if all the men would survive the night." Yet he reveals none of his misgivings, and shouts encouragement across the water.

In the morning, all of Shackleton's desperate crew members are still alive—and they get a break. The wind rises and shifts to the southeast. Shackleton decides to run west for Elephant Island, one hundred miles to the northwest. If the wind holds, they have a chance.

For three more days, the men and their boats battle the raging sea. Shackleton works to lift the spirits of his crew. At one point, he insists that photographer Frank Hurley wear his gloves after Hurley accidentally leaves his own pair on a floe. Another time, he calls out to Perce Blackborow, a stowaway the expedition leader has come to appreciate. Blackborow has no feeling in his feet; it seems only a matter of time before gangrene sets in. "We shall be on Elephant Island tomorrow," Shackleton tells him. "No one has ever landed there before, and you will be the first ashore."

Finally, on April 16, three battered lifeboats are hauled onto a lonely beach. Shackleton tries to keep his promise, but Blackborow cannot walk; two crewmen help him ashore. Another man collapses from a heart attack, but survives. For the first time in a year and four months, the expedition is on blessed land.

It is a victory, but Shackleton and his men know they are far from safe. Elephant Island is small and remote; no whaling ships will be stopping here. Shackleton soon announces that he and a party of five will set out for the whaling stations on the island of South Georgia. It is a truly desperate bid—sailing eight hundred miles in an open lifeboat on the planet's stormiest ocean to a piece of land twenty-five miles across at its widest. But Shackleton has no choice.

Shackleton selects his crew with care, considering not only the hard voyage ahead but also the plight of those left behind. Crack navigator Worsley is an obvious choice, and sturdy second officer Tom Crean and likeable seaman Tim McCarthy are also easy decisions. Two others—carpenter Harry McNeish and seaman John Vincent—are chosen as much for their rebellious nature as for their skills. Shackleton does not want them to poison the already grim environment they will leave behind on Elephant Island.

After making improvements to the *James Caird*, at twenty-two feet the expedition's largest lifeboat, Shackleton and his small band are off. Once again, their leader does what he can to make the journey bearable. Shackleton declares that there will be no swearing and establishes a schedule for meals, rest, watches, and manning the tiller. These measures are of little solace against mounting hardships, however. Layer after layer of ice weighs down the boat. One night, Worsley is frozen in position; the others have to unfold and massage him to get him into a sleeping bag. The wet bags begin to rot. Frostbite sets in.

Shortly after midnight on May 5, Shackleton is at the tiller. The sky is overcast and a gale is blowing. Shackleton looks up, sees a band of white, and calls to the others that the sky is clearing. A moment later he hears a low roar and looks up again. He realizes that the "clearing" is actually the crest of an enormous wave.

"Hold on!" he shouts. "It's got us!"

The seawater pounds the *James Caird* and everything in it, nearly tearing Shackleton from his seat. Though instantly flooded, the boat miraculously stays afloat. The men bail for their lives, knowing that any more water will sink them. Gradually, they rise out of the ocean again.

Three days later, having beat the incredible odds, McCarthy spies South Georgia. But before they can make a landing, a hurricane hits. The violent waves are too dangerous. With their goal only minutes away, Shackleton orders the boat back out to sea. After two more days of waiting, and with the crew's strength virtually gone, the *James Caird* makes for a small cove in the cliffs to starboard. The passage is narrow, but at 5 p.m. on May 10, Shackleton jumps ashore.

The harrowing adventure isn't over. The men have landed on the opposite side of the island from the whaling stations. They don't have the stamina for another 150-mile boat journey, nor do they want to risk being carried irretrievably into the Southern Ocean. They must attempt to cross the island—more than thirty miles of mountains, glaciers, frozen streams and lakes, and waterfalls—on foot. No one has ever done it.

At 2 a.m. on May 19, Shackleton, Worsley, and Crean set out under a full moon. Hoping to travel quickly, they carry no sleeping bags or stove. Their only climbing gear is a rope, nails hammered into their boots, and a carpenter's adze.

Three times the trio reaches the top of a ridge, only to be forced to retreat by some obstacle and search out a new path. Disheartened, they wonder if they will die here, alone in the middle of the island, after overcoming so much. Shackleton does not let them give up, however. "Come on, boys," he calls.

The sun is setting by the time the men reach the top of the fourth ridge. It is a steep, nine-hundred-foot slope down. They fashion a makeshift sled with the rope and, after a wild ride marked by screams and shouts, pick themselves up at the bottom of the slope. Amazingly, no one is hurt. They push on.

At seven the next morning, the trio hears sweet music in the distance: a steam whistle calling whalers to work. That afternoon, they reach the whaling station of Stromness and march to the manager's office.

Thoralf Sórlle knows Shackleton well but considers him lost somewhere at the bottom of the Weddell Sea. When he hears a knock at his door, he opens it to find three men in the most ragged clothing imaginable, their long hair matted and stiff, their faces black except for their eyes. Sórlle stares for a long moment.

"Who are you?" he says at last.

The man in the middle steps forward. "My name," he says in a quiet voice, "is Shackleton."

Three-and-a-half months later, after three attempts blocked by the ever-present ice, Shackleton is able to direct a ship to the familiar spit of land on Elephant Island. As they approach, Shackleton sees a group of disheveled men gathering on the beach, waving. A boat is lowered, and an impatient Shackleton climbs in.

Finally, the boat is close enough for Shackleton to be heard. "Are you all well?" he calls.

"All safe, all well" is the reply.

"Thank God!" The relief for Shackleton is indescribable. The grin on his face, however, says it all.

Would You? Could You?

(Share your answers if you're reading in a group)

Early polar exploration was no pleasure cruise for expedition leaders. Those who dared to search for the secrets of earth's ice-laden extremities were more likely to discover dissension, starvation, disease, insanity, and death. Charles F. Hall, captain of the first American attempt to reach the North Pole, was poisoned by his men in 1871. Adolphus Greely lost nineteen of his twenty-five men (including one he had executed) and was accused of cannibalism in the 1880s. Admiral Robert E. Peary's crew accused him of brutality and blamed him for at least one suicide in the 1890s. Robert F. Scott led his party of four to the South Pole, but all starved to death on the return trip in 1912.

Shackleton's expeditions were different. His men respected and almost revered him. They had full confidence in his decisions and ability to lead them out of trouble. Nearly a century later, despite falling short of every goal he originally set, Shackleton is universally admired. But what exactly was the quality of Shackleton's leadership? Does it still exist today? Do *you* have it? If you were in the same circumstances, *could you* have led Shackleton's men out of their incredible predicament on the Weddell Sea?

- How did Shackleton inspire his men to endure and work together? List some examples. Do you see any drawbacks to his approach?
- What are the qualities of great leadership? Which do you have? Which do you lack?
- What kind of leader was Jesus with his disciples? How was Shackleton the same? How was he different?
- Pastor and author Rick Warren has said that integrity and love are the biblical basis for leadership. Do you agree? Was this Shackleton's approach? Do you see evidence of this among our nation's leaders today? How about in your community? At your school or workplace?
- The Bible tells us that "The husband is the head of the wife as Christ is the head of the church," and "Husbands, love your wives, just as Christ loved the church and gave himself up for her to make her holy" (Eph. 5:23, 25–26). What does this mean to you in terms of leadership within a marriage and family?
- Who is the leader in your home? Do the principles that Shackleton applied to his men in the Antarctic also apply to your family? If not, what are the most important qualities for leading a family?
- Shackleton later wrote of the *Endurance* expedition, "I have no doubt that Providence guided us, not only across the snow fields, but across the storm-white sea that separated Elephant Island from our landing place on South Georgia. I know that during the long and racking march of thirty-six hours over the unnamed

201

mountains and glaciers of South Georgia, it seemed to me often that we were four, not three." How important do you think this sense of "Providence" was to Shackleton? What does it mean for any leader? Can a leader be effective without God's presence in his life?

Reporting In

Ask the Lord for new insight into what it means to be a leader. Pray that he will show you how to become the leader he designed you to be.

Hitting the Trail

(This is just for you)

Some of us are born leaders. Some of us would rather let others take the point. All of us face times when we are called to lead and when we are expected to submit to another authority. No matter where your comfort zone lies, you can do better.

- Make a list of your leadership roles, whatever they may be—student government officer, project coordinator, team captain, church youth leader, mentor. What can you change this week to become more like Shackleton—or, more importantly, like Jesus?

  _____

  _____

  _____

- Now list your subordinate roles. Are you the kind of team member who helps your leader accomplish goals? Does your leader see you as a valued partner or a malcontent? How would God have us respond to our leaders? (Hint: Read Ephesians 6:5–8.)

_____

_____

_____

- If you aren't already in a position of leadership, volunteer for a task that will give you the opportunity to develop your ability to lead. Keep a journal about your experience, either here or in a notebook.

_____

_____

_____

New Territory

(For those who want to explore further)

Watch the NOVA documentary *Shackleton's Voyage of Endurance* or read Alfred Lansing's *Endurance: Shackleton's Incredible Voyage*.

- What impressed you the most about Shackleton's leadership? When did he stumble, and how did he recover?
- Who else emerged as a leader on the expedition? Who displayed less admirable qualities? How would you have fared as a member of Shackleton's crew?

Resources

Chapter 1: Fear and Friendship at the Top of the World

Alexander, Eric. Interview by James Lund. September 16, 2009.

Farther Than the Eye Can See. DVD. Serac Adventure Films and Outside Television, 2003.

Greenfeld, Karl Taro. "Blind to Failure." *TIME*, June 18, 2001. http://www.time.com/time/magazine/article/0,9171,1000120,00.html.

Stoneman, Tonya. "Higher Summits." *In Touch*, June 2003.

Weihenmayer, Erik. "Tenacious E." *Outside*, December 2001.

Widdifield, Janna. "Journey to the Top of the World." *University of Denver Magazine*, Fall 2002, 17–21.

Eric Alexander's website, www.highersummits.com.

Chapter 2: Death and Birth in Blue John Canyon

Brick, Michael. "Climber Still Seeks Meaning in His Epic Escape." *New York Times*, March 31, 2009. http://www.nytimes.com/2009/03/31/sports/othersports/01ralston.html?_r=3&ref=sports.

"Being Aron Ralston," video, *New York Times*, http://www.nytimes.com/2009/03/31/sports/othersports/01ralston.html?_r=3&ref=sports.

Ralston, Aron. *Between a Rock and a Hard Place.* New York: Atria Books, 2004.

Survivor: The Aron Ralston Story (documentary). NBC News, 2006.

Chapter 3: Back on Board

Association of Surfing Professionals website, http://www.aspworld-tour.com/2009/index.asp.

Bethany Hamilton's personal website, www.bethanyhamilton. com.

Hamilton, Bethany. *Soul Surfer.* New York: Pocket Books, 2004.

John, Emma. "Riding the Storm." *The Observer*, June 28, 2009. http://www.guardian.co.uk/sport/2009/jun/28/bethany-hamilton-surfing.

Chapter 4: Not Without a Fight

Amazing Stories of Survival. From the editors of *People* magazine. New York: People Books, 2006.

Florida Department of Law Enforcement Speech, www.Tamara Brooks.org, http://iinspire.org/websites/tamarabrooks/pages/presentations.php.

Melero, Frank. Interview on *Larry King Live*, August 9, 2002. CNN. com transcripts, http://transcripts.cnn.com/TRANSCRIPTS/0208/09/lkl.00.html.

"To Hell and Back." *48 Hours Investigates*, August 27, 2003. http://www.cbsnews.com/stories/2003/01/31/48hours/main538761.shtml.

Chapter 5: Dance with Death

Kramps, B. J. Interview by James Lund. August 26, 2009.

Pierce, Todd. Interview by James Lund. July 9, 2009.

Peter, Josh. *Fried Twinkies, Buckle Bunnies, and Bull Riders.* Emmaus, PA: Rodale, 2005.

Professional Bull Riders website, www.pbrnow.com.

Chapter 6: A Brotherhood of Faith

Kurzman, Dan. *No Greater Glory.* New York: Random House, 2004.

The Four Chaplains: Sacrifice at Sea (documentary). DVD. Faith & Values Media, 2004.

The Four Chaplains Memorial Foundation. "The Saga of the Four Chaplains." http://www.fourchaplains.org/story.html.

Chapter 7: Blowup

Egan, Timothy. "Smokejumpers Face Summer's Fires with Memories of Last Year's Deaths." *New York Times*, May 29, 1995. http://www.nytimes.com/1995/05/29/us/smokejumpers-face-summer-s-fires-with-memories-of-last-year-s-deaths.html?pagewanted=all.

Junger, Sebastian. "Blowup: What Went Wrong on Storm King Mountain." *Fire Fighters.* New York: Thunder's Mouth Press, 2002.

Maclean, John N. *Fire on the Mountain.* New York: William Morrow & Company, 1999.

Useem, Michael. *The Go Point.* New York: Three Rivers Press, 2009.

US Forest Service. "Fire Behavior Associated with the 1994 South Canyon Fire on Storm King Mountain, Colorado." Research Paper RMRS-RP-9. http://www.fs.fed.us/rm/pubs/rmrs_rp009/4firechron.html.

Chapter 8: With Gladness

Burnham, Gracia. *In the Presence of My Enemies.* Wheaton: Tyndale, 2003, 2004.

Grinberg, Emanuella, and Eliott C. McLaughlin. "Former Hostages Reflect on Return to Normalcy." CNN.com, http://www.cnn.com/2008/US/07/03/former.hostages/index.html.

Olsen, Ted. "Martin Burnham Went Out Serving with Gladness." *Christianity Today*, June 1, 2002. http://www.christianitytoday.com/ct/2002/juneweb-only/6-10-11.0.html.

207

———. "Martin Burnham: Willing to Go." *Christianity Today*, July 8, 2002. http://www.christianitytoday.com/ct/2002/july8/17.19. html.

Chapter 9: Sailing the World at Seventeen

Friedman, Emily. "How Young Is Too Young to Risk Your Life?" ABC News, June 20, 2008. http://abcnews.go.com/International/Travel/Story?id=4966421&page=2.

Jones, Chris. "Do Hard Things." *ESPN the Magazine*, June 15, 2009. http://sports.espn.go.com/espn/page2/story?id=4233223.

Thomas, Pete. "Zac Sunderland, Solo Teen Sailor, Discovers Perils of the High Seas." *Los Angeles Times*, November 9, 2008. http://articles.latimes.com/2008/nov/09/sports/sp-zac9.

———. "Young Sailors, on Different Paths Around the World, Weigh Their Options." *Los Angeles Times*, May 29, 2009. http://latimesblogs.latimes.com/outposts/2009/05/young-sail ors-on-different-paths-around-the-world-weigh-their-options. html.

Wilson, Bernie. "Zac Sunderland's Around-the-World Sailing Journey Nears End." Associated Press, May 29, 2009. http://www.dailybreeze.com/news/ci_12479747.

Zac Sunderland's personal blog, www.zacsunderland.com/blog.

Chapter 10: Cold Night in the Elk Mountains

Colorado Avalanche Information Center website, http://avalanche.state.co.us/pub/info_faq.php.

Chapter 11: The Miracle Girl

Alderson, Jim. *Crash in the Jungle*. Cheltenham, U.K.: Nelson Thornes, 1979, 2001.

Gonzalez, Laurence. *Deep Survival*. New York: W. W. Norton and Company, 2003.

Leslie, Edward E. *Desperate Journeys, Abandoned Souls.* New York: Houghton Mifflin, 1988.

Pleitgen, Fredrik. "Survivor Still Haunted by 1971 Air Crash." CNN.com, http://www.cnn.com/2009/WORLD/europe/07/02/germany.aircrash.survivor/index.html.

Zullo, Allan, and Mara Bovsun. *The Greatest Survivor Stories Never Told.* Kansas City: Andrews McMeel Publishing, 2002.

Chapter 12: To the Last Breath

Kurson, Robert. *Shadow Divers.* New York: Random House, 2004.

NOVA. Hitler's Lost Sub. DVD. Lone Wolf Pictures, 2000, 2004.

Singer, Michelle. "Divers Tell Tale of Mystery Sub." CBSNews.com, September 2, 2005. http://www.cbsnews.com/stories/2005/09/01/60II/main811960.shtml.

John Chatterton's website, www.johnchatterton.com.

Chapter 13: Last Voyage of the *La Conte*

Lewan, Todd. *The Last Run.* New York: HarperCollins, 2004.

Noble, Dennis. *Great Rescues of the US Coast Guard.* Annapolis, MD: US Naval Institute Press, 2004.

Walker, Spike. *Coming Back Alive.* New York: St. Martin's Press, 2001.

Chapter 14: Boy Wonder

Abramowitz, Rachel. "Lessons Norman Ollestad's Father Taught Him." *Los Angeles Times*, June 12, 2009. http://articles.latimes.com/2009/jun/12/entertainment/et-norman-ollestad12.

CNN. Video interview with Norman Ollestad, June 30, 2009. http://www.cnn.com/2009/SHOWBIZ/06/30/plane.crash.survivor.book/index.html#cnnSTCVideo.

Ollestad, Norman. *Crazy for the Storm.* New York: HarperCollins, 2009.

Roberts, Robin, and Bonnie McLean. "Years after Plane Crash, Survivor Recalls Father." *Nightline* interview, ABC, June 3, 2009. http://abcnews.go.com/Nightline/story?id=7744392&page=1.

Chapter 15: Nightmare in Mogadishu

Bahe, Elizabeth. "Active Duty." *Worldwide Challenge*, January/February 2003.

Bowden, Mark. *Black Hawk Down*. New York: Signet, 1999, 2000.

"On the Set" bonus featurette. *Black Hawk Down*. DVD. Columbia Pictures, 2001.

Struecker, Jeff. *The Road to Unafraid*. Nashville: W Publishing Group, 2006.

Chapter 16: The Expedition

Lansing, Alfred. *Endurance*. Wheaton: Tyndale, 1999.

Morrell, Margot, and Stephanie Capparell. *Shackleton's Way*. New York: Viking, 2001.

NOVA. Shackleton's Voyage of Endurance. DVD. White Mountain Films/WGBH Educational Foundation, 2002.

Shackleton, Ernest. *South*. New York: Carroll & Graf Publishers, 1998.

Sullivan, Robert, and Robert Andreas. *The Greatest Adventures of All Time*. Des Moines: LIFE Books, 2000.

About the Authors

Peb Jackson is the principal of Jackson Consulting Group, assisting clients with public policy, development, public affairs, strategic mission needs, media, mentoring, and private-sector initiatives in Africa. He is the coauthor of *A Dangerous Faith* and a former executive with Spartan Oil, Azusa Pacific University, Focus on the Family, Generous Giving, Young Life, and Rick Warren. Peb is a regular adventurer, leading trips around the world, with many more tales yet to be told. He lives with his wife, Sharon, in Colorado.

James Lund is an award-winning freelance writer, editor, and author. He is the coauthor of *A Dangerous Faith* and the writer/collaborater on titles such as *Stronger* (with Jim Daly), *Going the Extra Smile* (with George Foreman), and *Bruchko and the Motilone Miracle* (with Bruce Olson).

A former newspaper reporter and editor and associate director of publications at Lewis & Clark College, Jim lives with his wife, Angela, and their three children in Central Oregon, where he enjoys occasional "adventuring" such as hiking and river rafting.

What do you think about the stories and themes in *Danger Calling*? Do you have a story to share about your call to risk and faith? We want to hear from you! Visit www.dangerous faith.net to send feedback and tell us about your adventure. You can also learn more about the authors and their work and read what others are saying about *Danger Calling*. We may even contact you about how your story can encourage others to risk for what really matters.

Share more true stories of adventure with your dad or your youth leader.

Includes eight brand-new stories not found in the youth edition.

When you become a *God Guy,* your life will never be the same.

A God Guy isn't just interested in God, he's connected to him.

YOUR FAITH IS LIKE A FIRE.
CONSIDER THIS YOUR BOX OF MATCHES.

Turn your daily devotions into an adventure.